"Billy Long has given to us a Biblica[l] work of the Holy Spirit for our everyo[ne] filled with Biblical references but also presents real-life experiences. I especially appreciate the balanced, practical application of the work of the Spirit. Wherever these principles are applied, the church is dynamic and growing thus confirming the presence and favor of God. I will purchase and distribute copies of this book because I believe it is desperately needed and will serve as a reliable guide to those who seek the Lord."

—CHARLES SIMPSON,
Chairman of the Board, CSM Publishing,
Author, *Straight Answers to 21 Honest Questions about Prayer,*
Internationally known Bible teacher and pastor

"…Take time to get acquainted all over again with the Person of the Holy Spirit and all of His gifts that are available to you. Billy Long has laid out a feast for you right here. Come and dine as the Master is calling!"

—DR. MARK CHIRONNA,
Church On The Living Edge
Mark Chironna Ministries

SPIRITUAL POWER

for

EVERYDAY LIVING

*Encounter the Holy Spirit
Like the Early Christians to
Reach Your Spiritual Potential*

BILLY LONG

HIGH BRIDGE BOOKS
HOUSTON

Spiritual Power for Everyday Living
by Billy Long

Copyright © 2016 by Billy Long
All rights reserved.

Printed in the United States of America
ISBN (Paperback): 978-1-940024-89-9
ISBN (eBook): 978-1-940024-90-5

High Bridge Books titles may be purchased in bulk for educational, business, fundraising, or sales promotional use. For information please contact High Bridge Books via www.HighBridgeBooks.com/contact.

Published in Houston, Texas by High Bridge Books

Unless otherwise indicated, all Scripture quotations are taken from the Holy Bible, New Living Translation, copyright © 1996, 2004, 2007 by Tyndale House Foundation. Used by permission of Tyndale House Publishers, Inc., Carol Stream, Illinois 60188. All rights reserved.

CONTENTS

FOREWORD

The early Church looked quite a bit different than the Church currently looks, particularly in the Western Culture. Long before the days of Constantine, when the Church became institutionalized, the Body of Christ was truly functioning as a priesthood of all believers, guided and directed by charismatically empowered traveling apostolic, prophetic, and evangelistic men and women whose sole purpose was to equip the saints to move in the charismatic power of the Holy Spirit and win the world for Jesus. The notion of only "leaders" functioning in power or in the charismata was not only foreign to Paul, Peter, John, Luke, and the rest, it was foreign to the called-out company of believers that were passionate followers of Jesus.

The Church multiplied and grew, quite simply because the saints and faithful were equipped by these charismatically gifted, itinerant equippers through whom, from house to house, all sorts of amazing things were happening. It doesn't mean the apostolic, prophetic, and evangelistically gifted equippers were not used mightily of God. That isn't the case. Indeed, they were. However, they saw their primary role as that of being facilitators and trainers, whose primary focus was on getting the New Covenant priests, the everyday followers of Jesus, to fulfill the Great Commission.

All the gifts of the Spirit were in operation in all of the believers' lives in the early Church. In fact, there is abundant evidence that the first eight centuries were replete with amazing manifestations of the power of the Spirit, all wrought not simply by the "leaders" of the movement called "The Church" but mostly by the everyday saints who did life together, broke bread together, and continued to give heed to the teaching of the charismatically gifted apostolic facilitators.

There is a desperate need for a recovery of the priesthood of all believers in the 21st century, not merely in word only but rather also in deed. It is one thing to confess and declare the priesthood of all believers; it is quite another to see the saints doing the work of the ministry so that the Body of Christ can be built up until we all come to the measure of the stature of the fullness that belongs to Christ!

Pastor Billy Long is a dear friend. I had the honor and privilege of co-laboring in the city of Raleigh, North Carolina as he facilitated the work God entrusted into his care and as I facilitated the work God entrusted into mine. For as long as I have known Billy, his passion has been for the Church to be equipped to move in the demonstration of the Spirit and power. He has never wavered in that regard, and he has contended for it continually. We share a common conviction that, without such an equipping, the Church will never fully accomplish what Jesus intended when He poured out the Holy Spirit for all to receive and clothed the original 120 with "power from on high".

That same Holy Spirit—the Third Person of the Holy Trinity and the Executive Agent of the Godhead here on Earth—is as available today as He always has been to fill the saints to overflowing so that they can abound in every good work. The book you now hold in your hands, *Spiritual Power for Everyday Living: Encounter the Holy Spirit Like the Early Christians to Reach Your Spiritual Potential* is the work of an apostolic co-laborer with Jesus whose sole desire is to see you come to the fullness of what Christ intends in your life.

Living the abundant life in and by the power of the Holy Spirit is the actual normal Christian life, not the substandard example that all too often is indicative of the average Church-goers today. Such Christians live far below their privileges and have been trained simply to go to a Sunday gathering and be about their own business for the rest of the week. Incarnating Christ in the culture is all about reliance on the indwelling Spirit to do those things in us that He did in the Last Adam, Jesus, when He walked the shores of Galilee. The works that He did, we are to do and in multiplied fashion. This isn't about one-man or one-woman ministries winning the world for Jesus. It is about a called-out company, the Church, the Ecclesia, fully prepared and thoroughly furnished to go about doing good and healing all who are oppressed by demonic powers.

The gospel is the power of God unto salvation, and Billy Long is inviting us to return to its simplicity as it was originally intended so that the fires of a new reformation can burn in the hearts of the faithful and so they can rejoice that, because their names are written in the Book of Life and because they have been endued with the Holy Spirit and power from on high, they can bring healing, deliverance, and release to those in need.

Take time to get acquainted all over again with the Person of the Holy Spirit and all of His gifts that are available to you. Billy Long has laid out a feast for you right here. Come and dine as the Master is calling!

DR. MARK J. CHIRONNA
Church On The Living Edge
Mark Chironna Ministries
Longwood, Florida

PROLOGUE

The first Christians "went out and preached everywhere, the Lord working with them and confirming the Word through accompanying signs" (Mark 16:20). The book of *Acts* is filled with examples of God's intimate presence and involvement in the life of the early Church. The Holy Spirit anointed the gospel message and presented Jesus Christ alive to those who heard the good news. The sick were healed, demons were cast out, and the dead were raised. The Church, with convincing power, bore witness to the resurrection of the Lord Jesus Christ.

The following chapters will give practical examples of God's miraculous intervention that many of my friends and I have witnessed with our own eyes. My desire is to stir spiritual hunger in those who are satisfied with dry routine and tradition and who have never witnessed the manifested presence of God working through His people by the precious work of the Holy Spirit. I also hope to rekindle the expectation and zeal of those who may have forgotten those wonderful days when they first experienced the power and presence of the Lord.

Part One defines spiritual gifts, gives practical examples, and exhorts the believer to stir his or her hunger for God's presence.

Part Two describes prophetic ministry as it functioned in the New Testament church.

Part Three gives in-depth teaching on praying in tongues and answers questions that are often asked about tongues.

Part 1

WHAT ARE SPIRITUAL GIFTS?

1

HUNGER FOR GOD'S PRESENCE

When I was a child, I marveled at the stories in the Bible. There was something in my heart that longed to see the manifestation of God's presence working intimately among His people. I wanted to experience the Lord's presence in the same way as did those people in the Bible. I especially remember sitting in a revival meeting in our Baptist church and feeling such frustration at how complacent and satisfied the people seemed to be. The Lord was with us; I knew that. But I felt so strongly that He wanted to do more and that He would surely come if we asked Him. I decided to do something about it.

When the pastor gave the invitation at the end of his message, I walked up to him and asked if I could say something to the congregation. He stopped the music, asked the congregation to be seated, and stepped back so I could speak. I am sure he thought it would be a good thing and "safe" to let a 16-year-old boy speak to the congregation.

Everyone listened intently. I looked over the crowd and said,

> I don't think we as a people are really praying and asking God to work among us. If each of us would actually take time to talk to the Lord before we come to these meetings... and ask Him to visit us... God would surely be here, revealing Himself

in some special way. I don't know what He would do, but I know He would do more than what we are seeing here now. As we sing another verse of the song, I want those of you who feel the same way to join me up front, and let's all kneel down here and ask the Lord to visit us.

The worship leader resumed the music, I knelt on the front row to pray, and about 25 or 30 people joined me. My heart rejoiced. People were responding. Something wonderful was happening. "Surely, there will be a change now," I thought. "The Lord may visit us in a special way tomorrow night." I naïvely thought the people would all go home and take some time to pray and that the pastor would be so happy about what I had done.

I was disappointed the next evening when I saw that everything was back to routine and that nothing had changed. I thought, "Obviously, not many... if any... are praying at home, and no one seems really hungry to see the Lord work among us beyond this ritual and routine." So, during the invitational song, I once again went up to the pastor and asked if I could say something. He very politely declined and said, "I think it would be best if you don't say anything tonight."

My heart sank. I realized then that he was satisfied with things the way they were. He was not interested in God "showing up" beyond the usual, and he especially did not want the congregation at the altar, praying on their knees. He was afraid of what might happen, and he was not about to allow a 16-year-old boy to instigate such activity.

A few months later, something happened to highlight the issue in my mind once again. During another revival meeting, a very well-dressed military man walked into the back of the auditorium during the worship. I saw him bend over and whisper to a gentleman on the back row who then arose and walked over to one of the families in the church and led them out to speak with this visitor. The pastor followed them out, and after a few minutes, he returned to the meeting and stood before the congregation to share the terrible news.

> The C___ family has just received news that their son's plane has been shot down in Vietnam, and he is now missing in action. Let's all come up to the front and pray for God to save this young man's life.

I watched as nearly the entire congregation gathered at the altar area to pray.

I asked the Lord,

> If this is the thing to do now… to break the routine, to gather in prayer to lift our voices together, to cry out for God's help in an emergency… why then do we not do it all the time? Why is it not a way of life? The world is full of emergencies and needs. People are always suffering everywhere. People are groping about and in need of God. People need the Lord. Why do we not sincerely and passionately call upon Him as part of our daily routine? Why is this not a part of our daily spiritual life as a people?

It blessed me to see the church in aggressive and passionate prayer during this time of need. But my question was, "Why do we not thirst like this every day? Why do we not thirst to know Him? To seek to walk intimately with the Lord daily… will this not strengthen our faith when we call upon Him during our times of need?"

Arise, cry out in the night, at the beginning of the watches; Pour out your heart like water before the face of the Lord. Lift your hands toward Him for the life of your young children...

—LAMENTATIONS 2:19

Oh, that you would rend the heavens! That you would come down! That the mountains might shake at your presence...

—ISAIAH 64:1

Oh God, You are my God; Early will I seek You; My soul thirsts for You; My flesh longs for You in a dry and thirsty land where there is no water. So I have looked for You in the sanctuary, to see Your power and Your glory.

—PSALM 63:1, 2

2

GOD'S PRESENCE: TO SEE OR NOT TO SEE

A little longer, and the world will see Me no more, but you will see Me...

—JOHN 14:19A

I was in the Spirit on the Lord's day, and I heard behind me a loud voice as of a trumpet... Then I turned to see the voice that spoke to me... and His countenance was like the sun shining in its strength...

—REVELATION. 1:10, 12, 16

...He rose again on the third day... and was seen... by Cephas, then by the twelve... by over five hundred brethren at once... He was seen by me also...

—1 CORINTHIANS 15:4, 5, 6, 8

The natural man comprehends God in the same way as a blind and deaf man would view a brilliant sunrise or listen to beautiful music. He would be oblivious to the wonders around him no matter how brilliant the sight or how loud the sound.

The revelation of God works on the same principle. The person who has a heart after God will see or hear Him through the smallest sign while the one who has rejected God in his heart will see nothing or will explain it away, no matter how powerful the Presence or how obvious the miracle. Jesus said that no sign would be given to an evil and adulterous generation (Matt. 12:39). He hides Himself from the proud but reveals Himself to the humble and to those who seek (1 Pet. 5:5).

It is amazing how those who reject God can close their eyes to His manifested presence.

The Pharisees knew firsthand that Jesus had raised Lazarus from the dead. They witnessed with their own eyes the awesome effects of this miracle on the people around Bethany and Jerusalem. They responded by plotting to kill Lazarus and silence his testimony (John 12:10).

The people of Israel trembled before the presence of God on Mt. Sinai, yet at the foot of this very mountain, they made a golden calf and fell into idolatry (Ex. 32:1-6).

Jesus rebuked certain cities where most of His mighty works had been done because they had refused to repent even in the face of such powerful evidence (Matt. 11:21-24).

Jesus told of the man in hell who begged "Father Abraham" to send someone back from paradise to warn his brothers not to come to "this place of torment." His argument was, "If one goes to them from the dead they will repent." The divine response was, "If they will not hear Moses and the Prophets (their Bible) neither will they be persuaded though one rise from the dead" (Luke 16:27-31).

The lesson is clear. The heart of man determines how he will respond to God's presence and initiatives. If he is inclined toward God, he will see the evidence and embrace the Lord. Otherwise, he will remain blind.

GOD'S PRESENCE HAS IMPLICATIONS FOR US

People often resist the presence of God because of the significance of its implications for them personally. The presence of God automatically shines a spotlight on our own natures. The more clearly we see God, the more clearly we know ourselves. This is one reason for our tendency to keep God at a safe distance away. When He shows up, we are forced to face certain realities in our lives. The manifested presence of God automatically creates a consciousness of our responsibility to respond to Him. If He shows Himself and we see Him, we have then lost our excuse for not seeking, serving, and obeying. At the same time, the more silent and distant God seems, the more we feel we can ignore Him in good conscience. But when He shows up, we are forced by His very presence to say "yes" or "no" to Him. Nominal Christians and people who are spiritually unresponsive are threatened by the manifested presence of God because it disturbs their complacency. And complacency is another form of saying "no" to God. To know Him greatly means to follow Him deeply. If He "stays away", then I can be lukewarm and live my life without being bothered. But if He shows up, I am then forced to deal with where I am in my relationship with Him.

Stephen was stoned because God showed up. The power of God was on Stephen so strongly that his words could not be resisted by the council before whom he stood. When stubborn and rebellious hearts encounter the irresistible words of God at this level, they cannot remain neutral, and they cannot hide underneath a cloak of pretense and complacency. Unable to resist Stephen's words, they either had to receive his words or kill him. They chose the latter. They actually stopped their ears and shouted loudly as they ran at him and stoned him to death (Acts 7:54, 57, 58a).

We should take note that the ones who resist God the loudest may be the very ones whose hearts are being pierced by the word God is speaking.

WHAT IS THE ATTITUDE OF CHURCHES TOWARD THE PRESENCE OF GOD?

In many cases, the attitude of churches can be described as follows. They want the Lord to be present, but they want Him to behave. They want Him close enough to keep watch but not close enough to be seen. They want God to be generally and mystically around but not specifically and pointedly obvious. They want Him to move in a general sense, quietly and unnoticed over an audience of passive spectators waiting to receive a warm feeling as they focus on what is happening up front on the platform.

Pastors want God to be present in the church but are often afraid of the risk involved in letting God show up in His people. They want God to work, but they don't want Him to use people. They are afraid of what might happen if the Holy Spirit is free to work through people in a supernatural way. Therefore, the agenda and programs tend to quench the working of the Holy Spirit. It is "safer" to prohibit than to learn from experience and actually lead.

We stand and pray for God to move among us, and we appeal to people to take initiative and be spiritually aggressive; at the same time, we create an atmosphere that prevents both. We quench the Spirit, and we do not allow people to express themselves genuinely. We want God to act but within our preset parameters. We want people to act but only in our precast organizational slots that exist to serve the institution. In other words, we ask God to show up and ask people to function; but, in reality, we are afraid of both.

WE SHOULD HUNGER FOR HIS PRESENCE

Since I was a teenager, I have never been able to understand why people who know and love God would not be passionately hungry and desirous to see Him and His works. Why would we be afraid of the miraculous visitations of His presence in our gatherings or out in the streets as we tell people about Jesus Christ who was crucified for our sins and is now alive and working among us by the power of the Holy Spirit? Why would we not be willing to take the risks involved in learning to be vessels through whom He can reveal Himself to a world that so desperately needs Him?

> *Oh that you would rend the heavens! That You would come down!... To make Your name known to your adversaries.*
>
> —ISAIAH 64:1A, 2B

> *And when they had prayed, the place where they were assembled together was shaken; and they were all filled with the Holy Spirit, and they spoke the Word of God with boldness... And with great power the apostles gave witness to the resurrection of the Lord Jesus. And great grace was upon them all.*
>
> —ACTS 4:31, 33

3

THE BAPTISM IN THE HOLY SPIRIT

And being assembled together with them, He commanded them not to depart from Jerusalem, but to wait for the Promise of the Father, "which," he said, "you have heard from Me; for John truly baptized with water, but you shall be baptized with the Holy Spirit not many days from now."... "You shall receive power when the Holy Spirit has come upon you; and you shall be witnesses to Me in Jerusalem, and in all Judea and Samaria, and to the end of the earth."

—ACTS 1:4-5, 8

After Jesus' resurrection, He met with the Disciples and told them to go into all the world and preach the gospel (Luke 16:15) but first to wait in Jerusalem until they were endued with power from on high (Luke 24:49). They waited in the Upper Room until the Holy Spirit was given on the Day of Pentecost (Acts 2:4). Following that, they went out with power, the Lord working with them and confirming the Word with signs following (Mark 16:20).

Much of the church world has lived between the Resurrection and Pentecost, having bypassed "the Upper Room" and gone forth without the supernatural power and presence and in the fullness God intended.

The baptism in the Holy Spirit is the "door" that moves us from living in the "foyer", opening the way into the many "rooms" of God's household that we have not yet experienced.

The first converts in the *Book of Acts* asked, "What must we do?" This was Peter's response:

> ...repent, and let every one of you be baptized [in water] in the name of Jesus Christ for the remission of sins; [born again] and you shall receive the gift of the Holy Spirit. For the Promise [baptism in the Holy Spirit) is to you and to your children, and to all who are afar off, as many as the Lord our God will call. (Acts 2:38-39)

Peter's answer is the same for us today. Jesus is *the* foundation of our faith and spiritual experience. But He has given to us three steps as foundational blocks for personal and church growth: be saved, be baptized in water, and be baptized in the Holy Spirit.

MY TESTIMONY

I had a major encounter with the Lord in the summer of 1966 just before my senior year of high school. Jesus revealed Himself to me in a very dramatic way and spoke clearly to my heart that He was calling me into the ministry. Word got around, and soon, I was getting invitations to speak at country Baptist churches throughout the area. During this time, I had heard that an outpouring of the Holy Spirit upon people was happening in all church denominations and around the world. People were being filled with the Holy Spirit and experiencing the power of God and the same miraculous works that we read about in the Bible, especially those in the *Book of Acts*. I was thrilled to hear this and began to study the Scripture verses dealing with the Holy Spirit.

Then, in April of 1967, I received the baptism in the Holy Spirit while my mother and I were praying for a friend. Kneeling and praying at a church altar, I sensed the presence of Jesus so intimately that it seemed I could reach out and touch Him. I stretched out my hands to the Lord and began to give thanks and praise. Suddenly, I began to pray in another language as the early Christians did on the Day of Pentecost, among Cornelius' household (Acts 10:44-46), and in other places in the New Testament. I was baptized in the Holy Spirit and knew this would be the beginning of a great adventure in my walk with the Lord and in His service.

I began to go about praying for people and actually saw people become healed. Jesus was more real to me than He had ever been, and I found a new freedom and release in my spirit to pray, to worship and praise, and to tell people about Jesus.

NEW BIRTH

The *new birth* is given to lost or unsaved people for the purpose of regeneration—that is, salvation. Jesus referred to salvation as a "fountain of water springing up unto everlasting life" (John 4:14). In the new birth, Jesus breathes the Holy Spirit upon the human spirit, causing a person to come alive in his fellowship and communion with God (John 3:3-8). Every Christian has the Holy Spirit in regeneration (Rom. 8:9).

BAPTISM IN THE HOLY SPIRIT

The baptism in the Holy Spirit then follows the new birth. Every Christian should ask the Lord to baptize him or her with the Holy Spirit. When a Christian is baptized in the Holy Spirit, he is not stepping into something strange and foreign to what he has already experienced. He is simply yielding more of himself to the presence and work of the Holy Spirit who has already come to him through salvation. The baptism in the Holy Spirit is given to believers, Christians, for the purpose of power and is like "rivers of water" flowing out of the Christian's innermost being (John 7:38-39). It is the door to spiritual gifts. When a person is baptized in the Holy Spirit, he is endued with power to witness for Christ and move in the supernatural manifestations of the Holy Spirit (1 Cor. 12:7-11). Being baptized in the Holy Spirit enables a person to release his own spirit with a new freedom in praise and worship.

EXAMPLES FROM THE *BOOK OF ACTS*

Pentecost (Acts 2:1-47)

The Holy Spirit was poured out on the believers as they waited in prayer and worship in the Upper Room. They were all filled with the Holy Spirit and praised the Lord in tongues (other languages) as the Holy Spirit gave them the utterance.

Samaria (Acts 8:4-17)

Philip, the evangelist, preached Christ to the Samaritans. Multitudes received Christ. There were many miracles as people were healed of various diseases, including those who were paralyzed and lame. Demons came out of many. There was great joy in the city. When the Apostles heard that Samaria had received the Word of God, they sent Peter and John to them who, when they had come, laid hands on them to receive the Holy Spirit.

The Apostle Paul (Acts 9:1-9, 17)

After Paul's conversion experience on the road to Damascus, he fasted and prayed, still blinded from the brightness of the vision he had seen. Jesus then sent a disciple named Ananias to him who laid hands on Paul and said,

> Brother Saul, the Lord Jesus who appeared to you on the road as you came, has sent me that you may receive your sight and be filled with the Holy Spirit.

Following this, Paul went forth to preach the gospel.

Cornelius' Household (Acts 10:44-48; 11:12-18)

While Peter was preaching at Cornelius' household, everyone present was filled with the Holy Spirit and spoke in tongues. Peter said,

> As I began to speak, the Holy Spirit fell upon them as upon us at the beginning (at Pentecost). Then I remembered the word of the Lord, how He said, "John indeed baptized with water, but you shall be baptized with the Holy Spirit."

Ephesus (Acts 19:1-6)

Paul came upon some believers in Ephesus. When Paul laid hands on them, the Holy Spirit came upon them, and they spoke with tongues and prophesied.

Other Examples (Gal. 3:2-5; Rom. 12:6; 15:18-19; 1 Cor. 12, 14; Heb. 2:3-4)

Although the *Book of Acts* itself does not give the accounts of other churches receiving the baptism in the Holy Spirit, we are certain that every church received the blessing. For example, the *Acts* makes no reference to Galatia, Rome, or Corinth receiving the gift of the Holy Spirit, yet the Apostle Paul—in his epistles to these churches—proves they had experienced the Holy Spirit by his references to "gifts", "spiritual gifts", "gifts of the Holy Spirit", "manifestations of the Holy Spirit", and "receiving the Spirit."

For All to Come (Acts 2:38-38)

The baptism in the Holy Spirit is for all believers of all time. After the first Christians were baptized in the Holy Spirit on the Day of Pentecost, Peter concluded his sermon with these words:

> Repent, and let every one of you be baptized in the name of Jesus for the remission of sins; and you shall receive the gift of the Holy Spirit. For the Promise is to you and to your children, and to all who are afar off, as many as the Lord our God will call.

WHY RECEIVE THE BAPTISM IN THE HOLY SPIRIT?

1. You will be obeying Jesus' command (Luke 24:49).
2. You will be following the pattern set by the first Christians in the *Book of Acts*.
3. It will make the presence of Jesus more real to you. It will help you to have more intimate fellowship with Him (John 14:16-21; 15:26).
4. It will empower you to be a more effective witness for Jesus Christ (Acts 1:8; 4:31-33; 5:32; John 15:26-27).
5. It will release your spirit to be more free in praise and worship (1 Cor. 14:14-18).
6. It will release your spirit to move in the manifestations of the Holy Spirit and to experience the power of God (1 Cor. 12:1; Acts 4:31, 33).
7. It will release you into more effective prayer and intercession (Rom. 8:26, 27; 1 Cor. 14:4).
8. It will release a greater sensitivity to the Holy Spirit to hear His voice and be led by Him.

9. It will cause the Bible to come alive to you because of the Spirit's presence to enlighten and because you can now identify with more of the Bible; you will understand it as being contemporary for today rather than relegating large portions of it as only for the first Christians.

10. It will help to intensify the purging process in your life (Luke 3:16-17).

11. It will lay the foundation for your spiritual growth.

OUR RESPONSIBILITY

The baptism in the Holy Spirit—that is, being filled with the Holy Spirit—releases in us the potential for all the wonderful things listed above. But we can be filled with the Holy Spirit and still not bear the fruit or walk in the gifts. The Holy Spirit does not force Himself or His works upon us. In order for the Spirit of God to produce in us and perform through us all of those things for which He is sent, it is necessary for us to receive Him in faith, present ourselves to Him, yield to Him, obey Him, and walk in Him. We hinder the Holy Spirit and prevent the fruit and gifts by resisting, quenching, and grieving the Holy Spirit (Acts 7:51; 1 Thess. 5:19; Eph. 4:30; Isa. 63:10).

BEING FILLED WITH THE HOLY SPIRIT

Repent... be baptized... and you shall receive the gift of the Holy Spirit..."

—ACTS 2:38, 39

The baptism in the Holy Spirit is not something you have to beg and plead for. It is a command to obey. God does not command something and then refuse it to us. This baptism is "for all who are afar off, as many as the Lord our God shall call." This means the Lord intends for every Christian to be filled with the Holy Spirit.

The baptism in the Holy Spirit is a "gift." A gift is received by grace, not merit. We do not earn a gift; it is free. If you had to earn it, it would not be a gift. You do not have to "become holy enough" to receive it. You simply have to be a disciple, a genuine Christian.

The baptism in the Holy Spirit is a "promise." A promise is a word that must be believed. A promise is received by faith, not by works. You do not "do things" in order to receive the promise. You simply believe the one who made the promise.

The baptism in the Holy Spirit is received like salvation— that is, by grace through faith (Eph. 2:7-8). If God shows such love, mercy, and grace to sinners by forgiving them, receiving them just as they are, and coming to live in them upon salvation, how much more will He fill with the Holy Spirit and empower those who are His and in whom He has already come to dwell (Rom. 5:1-10)?

WE CAN ASK AND RECEIVE WITHOUT FEAR

I have known people who were afraid to ask. They were worried about "getting the wrong thing"... as if the devil could throw an evil spirit into the event. The same Holy Spirit who comes to us in salvation comes to fill us when we are baptized in the Holy Spirit. The devil has no access or part in this. We must believe the words of Jesus:

> So I say to you, ask, and it will be given to you; seek and you will find; knock, and it will be opened to you. For everyone who asks receives,

and he who seeks finds, and to him who knocks it will be opened. If a son asks for bread from any father among you, will he give him a stone? Or if he asks for a fish, will he give him a serpent instead of a fish? Or if he asks for an egg, will he offer him a scorpion? If you then, being evil, know how to give good gifts to your children, how much more will your heavenly Father give the Holy Spirit to those who ask Him! (Luke 11:9-13)

HOW CHRISTIANS IN THE BIBLE RECEIVED THE HOLY SPIRIT

On the Day of Pentecost, believers were filled with the Holy Spirit while they were praying and worshipping (Acts 2:1-4). In Cornelius' household, they were attentively listening to a sermon (Acts 10:44-45). In other instances, the Holy Spirit was given through the laying on of hands (Acts 8:17; 9:17; 19:6).

DO I HAVE TO PRAY IN TONGUES?

Most Pentecostals and Charismatics believe that praying in tongues is the evidence of the baptism in the Holy Spirit. I will not be dogmatic on this point, but I do believe we should follow the example set for us in the *Book of Acts*. Although it might be possible for a person to be filled with the Holy Spirit without praying in tongues, I believe that everyone who is filled with the Spirit can and should pray in tongues. Praying in the Spirit opens up so many avenues in our spiritual life and serves so many useful and practical purposes. Should anyone fail to take advantage of this wonderful tool, he will fall short of his spiritual potential and will miss available opportunities provided by the grace of God.

Part Three of this book will help you to understand the significance and importance of "praying in the Spirit."

4

DEFINITIONS OF THE
HOLY SPIRIT'S MANIFESTATIONS

*Now concerning spiritual gifts, brethren, I do not want
you to be ignorant... But the manifestation of the Spirit
is given to each one for the profit of all...*

—1 CORINTHIANS 12:1, 7

It is fitting that the Apostle Paul begins his discussion of
spiritual gifts by expressing his desire that the church not be
ignorant of them. This statement implies there is knowledge
and understanding to be gained beyond a casual reference or
quick dismissal of the subject. It also implies the apostle knew
that, despite the pervasiveness of the supernatural working of the
Holy Spirit in the early Church, there would be the possibility of
spiritual *gifts* being either neglected or abused. His concern is
valid today and should motivate us to search out knowledge,
understanding, and experience.

We can learn much from teaching, but experience is
necessary to really understand the manifestations of the Holy
Spirit. Jesus taught by word and by example. The disciples
learned by listening to His words, watching Him in action, and
practicing what He taught and modeled. Trying to understand

the manifestations of the Holy Spirit without experiencing them is like trying to be an automobile mechanic just by reading the manual. It requires not only study but also training. The Bible is our manual and is absolutely foundational, but James tells us to "be doers of the Word and not hearers only" (Jam. 1:6). Experience gives substance and weight. Without it, we would remain in the arena of intellectual discussion and doctrine. The Apostle Paul said the gospel did not come in word only but also in power and in the Holy Spirit (1 Cor. 2:4).

"CHARISMA"

The Greek word *charisma* is translated "gift" and is rooted in the word for "grace." It refers to a broad range of spiritual gifts and, by definition, signifies they are the operations of God's grace. *Charismata* (spiritual gifts) encompass three main areas: offices, ministries, and manifestations. Here is a general definition of each.

1. **Offices:** Office gifts are given to equip and strengthen the Body of Christ. They include apostles, prophets, evangelists, pastors, and teachers and are special callings (Eph. 4:11).

2. **Ministries:** There are various, specialized areas of service that are, in fact, ministries but not offices. These include teaching, ministries of miracles, healing ministries, serving, giving, prophesying (not the office of prophet), administrations, etc. (Rom. 12:6-8). All Christians can have ministries or areas where they are gifted to serve.

3. **Manifestations:** Manifestations of the Holy Spirit are listed in 1 Corinthians 12:7-11. Paul lists nine ways in which the Holy Spirit manifests Himself:

    -   The word of wisdom
    -   The word of knowledge
    -   Faith
    -   Healings
    -   Miracles
    -   Prophecy
    -   Discerning of spirits
    -   Tongues
    -   Interpretation of tongues

Any Spirit-filled Christian can potentially move in any or all of the nine manifestations of the Spirit as they are needed. These operations of the Spirit do not refer to specialized ministries or one gift that a person carries around with him but rather to a variety of ways the Holy Spirit may use any believer at any time as He chooses or as the need arises.

It is also important to note that the terms in this list refer to specific, supernatural acts of the Holy Spirit and not to natural human talent or acquired skill. For example, the "word of knowledge" does not refer to "knowledge" in general but rather to a "word" of knowledge. Jesus' word to the woman at the well is a good example.

MANIFESTATION

The term *manifestation* used in 1 Corinthians 12:7 means that the Holy Spirit comes to reveal Himself as the presence of Christ at work through His people. He is not a vague, distant, impersonal presence. He is not just a doctrine, or emotions, or some nice concept we refer to in our liturgy. He is the active presence of God revealed. Peter described Him as "this which you now see and hear" (Acts 2:33). Paul described Him as the "demonstration of the Spirit and power" (1 Cor. 2:4). The Holy Spirit desires to carry us beyond empty ritual and theology to bear witness to the resurrection of Jesus Christ in tangible ways. This happens when we present ourselves to Him and allow Him to work.

DEFINITIONS OF THE NINE MANIFESTATIONS

A Word of Wisdom

This does not refer to wisdom in general but to a specific word of wisdom for a specific situation, a special word given to help in a difficult situation or a time of perplexity. It does not refer to philosophical wisdom but to practical wisdom, helping us to know what to do, how to do something, or what to say. It is a word that clarifies and gives divine perspective in a matter.

A Word of Knowledge

As noted above, this refers to a special word of knowledge, not to general knowledge acquired through study or by efforts of the natural mind. It is a supernatural knowing.

There are many examples of this is the lives of the Old Testament prophets, Jesus, and the Apostles.

Faith

There are three categories of faith:

- *Faith dealt to every Christian, the faith involved in salvation*: Romans 12:3 says that God has dealt to each one a measure of faith.

- *Faith which is a general trust and confidence in God*: This faith is revealed in how we face life in our daily walk with God.

- *Faith that is a manifestation of the Holy Spirit as listed in 1 Corinthians 12:9.*

Faith as a manifestation of the Holy Spirit does not refer to the usual or general faith that is always active and present with the Christian but to a special faith for a specific purpose. It refers to a surge of confidence given for a particular need or circumstance. It is the supernatural emptying of doubt as a person, by divine revelation, receives clear insight into the knowledge of God's will and purpose regarding a matter, resulting in the absolute certainty that it will come to pass. It involves special insight into the will of God with the certainty that it will be done. This insight is accompanied by the grace to either pray it or speak it into completion. This type of faith produces outstanding and unusual events. Here are a few examples:

- Matthew 17:20
- Acts 6:8
- Mark 5:28
- Acts 14:8-10
- Hebrews 11: The heroes of faith all moved in a general faith and trust in God, but many also moved in special faith for outstanding and unusual events.

Healing

Healing is a supernatural working of the Holy Spirit to cure sickness and disease in the name of Jesus. This was a common occurrence in the early Christian Church. Jesus commissioned the Church to heal and then placed healing in the Church as one of the manifestations of the Spirit. The following healing methods were used in the Bible: prayer, laying on of hands, anointing with oil, speaking the word of faith, simply believing, the use of handkerchiefs or aprons, having the sick person do something (such as wash or dip in water), and touching the garment or shadow of one anointed with healing ministry.

Miracles

Miracles can be defined as God's using someone to do the impossible or various supernatural works. Miracles in the Bible include the dead being raised, food multiplying, walking on water, special healings, creative miracles, limbs restored, and miracles of provision.

Prophecy

Prophecy in the New Testament Church was not "preaching." Prophecy is speaking by immediate revelation and by inspiration of the Holy Spirit. It can relate to past, present, or future. The time aspect is not primary, but rather it is the Lord speaking to encourage, comfort, strengthen, or to bring some revelation. Prophecy is the Holy Spirit's moving upon a person to speak a word from God to a specific person or group of people. It can be an intense and dramatic word or a quiet and gentle word to remind someone that God loves them.

There are three levels of prophecy:

- **The office** of a prophet (Eph. 4:11; Acts 21:10-12)
- **The ministry** of prophecy in which a person is specially gifted in ministering to others prophetically (Rom. 12:6; Acts 21:9)
- **The manifestation** of the Holy Spirit: "You can all prophesy." (1 Cor. 14:24, 31)

Discerning of Spirits

This is supernatural revelation that gives one the ability to discern (recognize and know) what type of spirit is at work in a person or situation. It is the ability to know if the source is God (of God), an evil spirit (of Satan), or the human spirit (of man).

Another aspect of this particular gift is the ability to discern a person and his character. Jesus demonstrated this type of discernment many times as He "saw" or discerned the nature, character, and motivation of people around Him. This gift operates when it is specifically needed and when the Holy Spirit chooses. It is not intended to cause one to be critical, condemning, or always trying to judge others.

Tongues

"Tongues" ("languages") is the supernatural ability to pray in another language (either earthly or heavenly) by means and inspiration of the Holy Spirit. When praying in tongues, a person's spirit is praying. It can be intercession or praise and worship. It strengthens the believer and builds him up. This type of tongues does not need an interpreter, and there is no limit to the number of people who can worship or pray together in this manner. All of the examples of tongues given in *Acts* are of this type. In each of these occasions, there are more than "three at the most" who are praying in tongues. Every Christian can pray in the Holy Spirit in intercession and praise.

A second type of tongues is the message given to the church or a prayer in tongues given before the church. In this case, an individual is moved to speak a message in tongues while the church listens quietly. This is to be interpreted and is limited to two or three at the most.

Interpretation of Tongues

The interpretation of tongues is Holy Spirit's giving someone an interpretation of or response to a message previously given in tongues. There are varying opinions as to the nature of the interpretation. It may be a literal translation of a message given in tongues to the church or possibly a prophetic response to a prayer in tongues given before the church.

PURSUE LOVE AND DESIRE SPIRITUAL GIFTS

The gifts are for every believer and not just for some special person up front on stage. They may be spectacular, but they usually will reflect the quiet and gentle moving of the Holy Spirit as Christians reach out to one another with compassion and care.

When we speak of spiritual gifts, we are speaking of the presence of Jesus Christ working among us. We are not necessarily focusing on the spectacular and the dramatic although these do occur from time to time. But mostly, we look for those unobtrusive and often unnoticed acts of the Holy Spirit working in the background and which flow among us as life and grace, quietly yet deeply touching and blessing the lives of those around us. It is those daily, obscure, and non-spectacular acts of obedience that strengthen the Church. It flows out of the individual's desire to be used of God and his or her willingness to reach out to people in church and in the marketplace with love and compassion.

Pursue love, and desire spiritual gifts.

—1 CORINTHIANS 14:1A

5

THE BIBLICAL CONTEXT FOR THE SUPERNATURAL

There are three common errors in how churches approach the manifestations of the Holy Spirit. Evangelical churches tend either to dismiss them (ignoring them altogether) or to naturalize them (doing away with the supernatural aspect). Pentecostal denominations, which claim acceptance of the gifts, have often quenched them through emotionalism.

The error of the non-Christian world is that it imitates spiritual gifts through psychic and occult phenomena, which are demonic counterfeits of the true. When man seeks spiritual experience apart from the God of the Bible, he will encounter human soul power and evil spirits. In modern cultures, evil spirits have masqueraded as "good" and have lured many educated folk into the pantheistic world of the New Age movement. In our modern culture, the spirit realm has disguised itself as "good" and gives people spiritual experiences with "warm fuzzies" included. The devil comes as an angel of light.

Pagan and primitive societies have been generally animistic, either worshiping spirits or seeing them in everything. They know the reality of spirits and their malevolent nature. They generally fear them and constantly try to placate them through their religious rites and cultural practices. With the exception of modern New Age philosophies that see good spirits in inanimate objects and nature, most primitive societies have always recognized the unmasked evil in the spirit realm and have lived in fear of these spirits for what they really are.

American culture has seen a rise of activity in the non-Christian supernatural realm through New Age, Eastern mysticism, occult, and psychic phenomena. Multitudes have sought spiritual reality while attempting to avoid the God of the Bible and the moral demands He places upon His followers. This has resulted in a rise and acceptance of various facets of Eastern religions with their New Age practices, including yoga and meditation—which seem harmless on the surface but are demonic in their origins—a fascination with the occult and paranormal phenomena, astrology (horoscope), and witchcraft. All of these practices introduce people to the demonic, supernatural realm.

The Bible forbids our involvement with such practices because they represent a form of idolatry, they introduce people to the realm of evil spirits, and they counterfeit the manifestations of the Holy Spirit as taught in Scripture.

THE BIBLICAL CONTEXT FOR THE SUPERNATURAL: JESUS, THE BIBLE, AND THE CHURCH

The genuine manifestations of the Holy Spirit occur within an atmosphere where Jesus Christ is glorified as Lord and the Bible is respected as the Word of God. People are filled with joy and peace as they are healed, set free, encouraged, and strengthened. True Christians need not fear nor be apprehensive about the workings of the Holy Spirit. Within the context of the guidelines given below, Christians can discern what is of God and what is of the evil one.

Lordship of Jesus

The supernatural must be within the context of the people who confess and follow Jesus Christ as Lord and Savior.

The New Testament is very clear. The Holy Spirit comes to reveal and glorify Jesus Christ as Lord. Jesus affirmed this to His disciples before He ascended to the Father (John 15:26). The *Book of Acts* is filled with examples of the supernatural manifestations of the Holy Spirit as He reveals Christ and confirms the Gospel message with miracles, healings, exorcisms, prophetic utterances, and great joy. The letters of the apostles reaffirm and establish as foundational the truth that those under the influence of the Holy Spirit will acknowledge and confess that Jesus is Lord. These writers also stated that anyone working in the supernatural who does not acknowledge the Lordship of Jesus is a false prophet and of the Antichrist (1 John 4:1-3; Rev. 19:10; 1 Cor. 12:1-3).

The Bible

The supernatural must be within the context of the biblical model—that is, within the context of those who believe the Bible to be God's Word and who walk according to it, both doctrinally and morally. The supernatural must follow the pattern found in the Gospels, the writings of the apostles, and in the *Book of Acts*.

The biblical writers exhorted God's people to trust only those whose message was according to their written Bible. Moses warned Israel to reject any prophet or miracle worker who spoke contrary to the written Law and Word of God that Moses had given (Deut. 13:1-3).

Isaiah warned Israel of those who claimed supernatural gifting but who did not speak according to the Law and testimony given by Moses and the prophets (Isa. 8:19-20).

The Apostle Peter tells us that the written Word of God is more sure than a voice from heaven and that we would do well to heed it as a light that shines in a dark place (2 Pet. 1:12-21).

The Church

The supernatural must be within the context of the church, the people of God who confess Jesus Christ as Lord. We are referring to people and not to buildings or corporate entities; we are referring to the living Body of Christ that transcends all political and corporate entities.

The context of the Church refers to followers of Christ functioning under the authority of God's Word, believers gathered in His name, as well as those involved in personal ministry and outreach in daily life as they interact with the world outside the church.

In 1 Corinthians 11-14, the Apostle Paul speaks of the gifts of the Holy Spirit working within the context of the Body of Christ, the Church. Paul tells us that "God has appointed them in the church" (1 Cor. 12:28). Paul lists the manifestations of the Holy Spirit as well as ministry gifts in 1 Corinthians 12 and in Romans 12:4-8. He discusses these gifts within the context of the Church, the Body of Christ.

The Holy Spirit comes to reveal and glorify Jesus. A "manifestation" of the Holy Spirit is actually a manifestation of Jesus Himself, walking among us and working through us. For the Church to express the fullness of Christ to this world, it must abound and grow in both the fruit and gifts of the Holy Spirit (Eph. 4:13). The fruit of the Holy Spirit (Gal. 5:22-23) expresses the nature of Christ, His love and holiness. The gifts or manifestations of the Holy Spirit (1 Cor. 12:7-12) express the power and actions of Christ. This is the true biblical context for the supernatural, an atmosphere where followers of Christ walk in His Word and express His nature and power by the fruit and gifts of the Holy Spirit.

6

FAITH, LOVE, AND SPIRITUAL GIFTS WORK TOGETHER

People who reject the supernatural working of the Holy Spirit in the Church today often tend to emphasize "faith" and "love" as substitutes for and reasons to eliminate the supernatural works of the Holy Spirit. This logic sounds spiritual but is inconsistent with the life and ministry of Jesus, the practices of the New Testament Church, and the ministry of the apostles. The following, which was written by an acquaintance of mine, is an example of this type of thinking:

> The trial is to walk in faith alone… no miracles… faith alone… that is the true miracle to stay strong without inventing additional reasons to be blessed. He said so himself… I am the way. Through me is salvation, period. No debate… and that we will have to live on faith alone… no miracles… no tongues… no gimmicks… faith alone.

On the surface, these words sound spiritual, but a logical reflection will show the error of such thinking and how inconsistent it is with the very Scripture my friend uses to support his position.

The concept of "faith alone" is found in Paul's letters and in Peter's preaching. It means we are saved by faith alone rather than by works or merit. But "faith alone" for salvation does not eliminate its other functions and its role in the supernatural working of the Holy Spirit. Faith permeates every area of our Christian walk. It is the instrument of salvation. It sustains us in our daily walk and when it seems God's presence is far away. It also releases the supernatural works of the Holy Spirit.

Jesus said to the Canaanite woman, "O woman, great is your faith! Let it be to you as you desire." And her daughter was healed in that very moment (Matt. 15:28).

The Scripture also says that Jesus could do no mighty work in His hometown because of their unbelief (Matt. 13:58).

The Apostle Paul said,

> Therefore He who supplies the Spirit to you and
> works miracles among you, does He do it by the
> works of the law, or by the hearing of faith?
> (Gal. 3:5)

Faith invites God's miraculous presence; it does not remove the need for it.

Jesus' statement, "I am the way" (John 14:6a), was not meant to contradict or do away with His miraculous works. Obviously, He was performing miracles, healing the sick, and casting out demons in the very context in which these words were spoken. Jesus did not say to the multitudes, "I am the Way. Because it is by faith alone, I, therefore, will not work miracles."

The early Christians walked in the supernatural gifts of the Holy Spirit and recognized them as God's very presence at work. They did not consider these experiences to be gimmicks. We should be as comfortable with the supernatural presence of God as were those first followers of Christ.

SPIRITUAL GIFTS AND LOVE

Pursue love, and desire spiritual gifts.

—1 CORINTHIANS 14:1A

So many people approach the subject of the manifestations or gifts of the Holy Spirit from a purely doctrinal or analytical point of view. Doing this is to miss the real significance and wonder of it all. A person's ability to fully appreciate the magnificent gifts and tools the Lord has placed in his or her hands depends on the depth of his or her vision and motivations. What a person sees will determine what he or she reaches for. What a person desires (and why he or she wants it) determines the passion and enthusiasm with which he or she pursues it.

The Apostle Paul covered the issues of desire and motivation when he said we should "pursue love and desire spiritual gifts" (1 Cor. 14:1). When we move in the manifestations of the Holy Spirit, we are expressing our hunger for God's active presence among us, and we are showing our love and care for those around us. Jesus healed people because He was moved with compassion. Likewise, we will move in the gifts of the Spirit as we are moved with His compassion. The gifts, therefore, are instruments of God's love.

I want to move in prophetic insight because there are people who need an encouraging word from God. I want to have a word of wisdom because someone is perplexed or confused and asking God for direction. I want to see miracles because so many people are facing impossibilities and need the "waters to part." I want to pray in the Spirit because it strengthens my prayer life, strengthens my spirit, and helps to release my ability to move in the other gifts of the Spirit, which will result in others being touched with the compassion, presence, and power of God.

When we speak of spiritual gifts, we are speaking of the presence of Jesus Christ working among us by the Holy Spirit to touch and bless others with His love and compassion.

7

MRS. BERTHA DANCES – ERNEST DOES THE TWIST

It was the summer of 1969. I was 20 years old. My friend, Larry Rodeffer, and I had just finished our second year of college at Oral Roberts University and were preaching revivals during the summer in Ohio, Kentucky, South Carolina, North Carolina, Virginia, and West Virginia. On this tour, we held a series of meetings for nine nights in my home community of Longs, South Carolina. We used the Ebenezer Methodist Church building. Though thriving and growing today, it was abandoned with no congregation at that time, but it was in good condition and maintained by a family who hoped to see church activities revived again someday. Larry and I were granted permission to use the facility for our meetings.

The little church building was filled almost to capacity with about 80 people attending our meetings nightly. The atmosphere was electric, and people came expecting to see the hand of God at work. Larry and I preached the gospel, sharing the good news that Jesus Christ died for our sins and was raised from the dead as Lord of all. We proclaimed that He had sent the Holy Spirit as His living presence among us to reveal Himself. "He is here now to save and to heal!" we proclaimed. Great faith arose in the hearts of the people, and the presence of God moved over the congregation.

One Baptist lady, Mrs. Bertha, came to the meetings with a very serious back problem. She complained that she was unable to do any gardening or housework because of the affliction. She stood before me, praying silently and expecting something from God. I asked Jesus to touch her and laid my hands on her head. She immediately raised both of her arms straight up toward heaven, began to cry with joy, and started dancing. The Lord had instantly touched her and healed her back. She later told me how she had gone home from that meeting and had begun doing garden work and housework the next day with no pain.

As I walked into one of the meetings, I saw a young man seated and wearing a back brace. He had been in a car accident and had broken his back. As I walked past him, he looked up and said, "I'm expecting God to heal me tonight."

I responded, "If you're expecting it, you'd just as well get ready for it," as I walked up to the platform.

When I had finished preaching, Ernest came to the front for prayer. When I laid my hands on his head, he began to cry, saying, "I'm healed! I'm healed!" He then went outside, removed the back brace, and began bending over and twisting around. He was healed. He went to his doctor in Loris, South Carolina, who confirmed the healing.

There were other testimonies of God's intervention in the lives of people during those meetings. One lady was healed of psoriasis. Another was healed of a tumor. Larry and I were just 20 years old at the time and were moving in a child-like faith. We simply expected God to show up.

Great grace was present to bring forth faith in the people, and we rejoiced to see lives touched and changed. But the greatest joy of those days was the strong sense of the presence of Jesus Christ. It was as if He was physically walking among us.

In one of the meetings, I turned to see a little six-year-old girl standing to the side and softly crying. "Are you okay? What is happening?" I asked.

She looked at me with tears in her eyes and said, "Jesus is in this place. Jesus is in this place." He was revealing Himself, even to the children.

I remembered the words of Jesus:

> ...the world will see Me no more, but you will see Me... And he who loves me will be loved by My Father, and I will love him and manifest myself to him. (John 14:19a, 21b)

8

PAPA'S MIRACLE

Tharon Hardee was my maternal grandfather. The grandchildren called him "Papa". In 1964, he was in his seventies and was a member of a church but was living a life inconsistent with his Christian testimony. I was 15 years old at the time and remember sitting in Papa's family room and listening intently as my mother, her sisters, and her brother expressed to him their concerns about his eternal soul.

"Daddy," they told him, "we are worried about you and are concerned that you are not walking with the Lord as you know you should."

"Why? Jesus is my all in all!" he responded emphatically and acted surprised that they would question his behavior. He was not ready to admit the truth about where he was, and it seemed that the discussion had no apparent effect. He continued his life on the same course, doing the things he knew were displeasing to the Lord.

A few months later on a Saturday evening while I was at my weekend job of steaming oysters at a local seafood restaurant, I received word that Papa had had a stroke and was in critical condition and that I should go immediately to Loris Hospital where the family was gathering. I entered the emergency room just as they were pushing him down the hall. As his bed was rolled past me, he looked up at me with distress in his eyes and with heavily slurred speech said, "Billy, pray for me!" This cry told me that, in his heart, he knew the reality of what his children had been trying to tell him. Facing death, he had to face the truth.

"Okay, Papa," I said as they rolled him past me and on to treatment.

He was in the hospital for about three weeks but finally recovered enough to be sent home. He was alive, but the stroke had left him unable to walk. The family decided I should sleep at my grandparents' home at night in order to help my grandmother care for him. I would lift him up off of his bed every morning and literally carry him to the little cot that had been placed in the family room where he would remain all day. In the evenings, I would go back to his house to resume my duties helping my grandmother. How well I remember going over to that little cot each night, lifting him up, carrying him in my arms, and placing him in his bed where he would sleep for the night. This routine went on for about two weeks.

Then one Saturday, his nephew, Carl, came by to pray for him. He read 2 Chronicles 7:14, and the verses leapt from the pages almost like an audible word from God to my grandfather. Every word seemed to be a word directly from God. They described him perfectly, stating the problem and the solution.

> If my people who are called by my name will humble themselves and pray and seek my face, and turn from their wicked ways, then I will hear from heaven, and will forgive their sin, and will heal their land.

Carl read the Scripture, said the prayer, and then left. Papa, sitting alone on that cot with those words echoing in his heart, looked up to the Lord and took Him at His Word. He repented and turned his life over to the Lord in that very moment.

A few minutes later, my mother received a phone call from my grandmother saying, "Jessie Lois, Tharon wants you to come here now." When Mama and I walked in, we saw Papa sitting on his cot crying. With tears streaming down his cheeks, he looked up and said, "Lois, the Lord has restored to me the joy of my salvation." After a pause, he continued, "And I think He has healed me, too."

Mama then shouted, "Well, get up, Daddy!"

He immediately arose and began to walk. He was crying and laughing at the same time, rejoicing in the overwhelming knowledge of God's forgiveness, joy, and healing. I still remember him walking out the back door and circling the house a couple of times with his arms lifted, praising and thanking the Lord for his healing. My mom and I immediately called the rest of the family to tell them of the miracle.

Papa was a new man after that. I remember being with him when friends from his past who had not heard of his transformation would come up to him and make some crude comment or some reference to his past life. He would get a very serious and stern look on his face. "I don't do that anymore," he would say and then explain to them that he was walking with the Lord now and that his life had changed. I watched him love the Lord and walk with the Lord until the day of his death about two years later. Whenever I would visit him during those two years, he would always ask me to pray for him and with him before I left. Often, at night, I would sit with him and read to him from the Bible. Those are precious memories. I had witnessed his years of hypocrisy and then had the joy and privilege of witnessing his wonderful healing and the transformation that came to him when he faced reality and was honest with himself before God. We can all learn a lesson from this.

> *But... the good ground are those who, having heard the Word with an honest and good heart, keep it and bear fruit with patient endurance.*
>
> —LUKE 8:15

Behold, you desire truth in the inward parts…

—PSALM 51:6A

9

MY VISIT TO A PHILOSOPHY OF RELIGION CLASS

Agirl from our church in Raleigh, North Carolina was taking a philosophy of religion class taught by a professor from Duke University. Nancy came to me one evening and shared how she had been brought to tears when some of the other students mocked her for sharing her faith during a class discussion. Nancy was a committed Christian and loved the Lord. She was shocked at the unbelief and skepticism of the professor and the students and soon came to discuss it with me and fellow believers at church.

Now, she was asking me to visit the class. The professor had told the students to invite their pastors to come sit in on the discussions. My first thought was, "This professor wants to pull out all his weapons of complex, intellectual, theological, and philosophical thought and esoteric terms to make me or any other pastor who shows up look like an idiot in front of the class." But I knew this was a great opportunity, so I agreed to go.

The next week, one of the men from the church went with me to the class. I was a little nervous as we took our seats but was filled with faith, knowing the Lord wanted us there.

After the professor opened the class and welcomed me and Colin, he addressed me with the following question: "In light of..."

At this point, he began very eloquently using many "ten-dollar" words, rare theological terms, and historical names hardly known to the common layman, the meaning of which was very difficult to follow. At first, I thought he was deliberately trying to use academic, esoteric terms to confuse me so that I would not be able to answer his question intelligently. But then, to my surprise and great delight, he concluded his thoughts with the following question:

> Jesus and the apostles are said to have worked miracles. Therefore, because you teach your people that the Bible is true, what do you say to your parishioners who ask you why we do not see miracles today?

This professor thought he was dealing with a dispensational cessationist, a person who believes the Bible but also believes miracles have ceased. This cessationist base is a weak position on which to stand in the face of an articulate, liberal philosopher who sees it as illogical and irrational religious hypocrisy. They conclude that, if they don't see miracles happening now, they never did.

My response to this professor shocked him and the whole class. I answered,

> We teach that the Bible is true and that Jesus died for our sins, was raised from the dead, and is alive today… and that He has given us His Holy Spirit as His living and active presence with us. So, when people ask me why we do not see miracles today, I tell them, "Hang around here a while, and you will see one!"

You could have heard a pin drop as I proceeded to share testimonies of healings and miracles that I and others in our church had either witnessed or been a part of. I gave examples of supernatural healings, exorcisms, and examples of the workings of the Holy Spirit as listed in 1 Corinthians 12.

The same students who had scorned Nancy's testimony before were now sitting there silent and amazed. Suddenly, one of them spoke up and said to the professor, "The way it looks to me... you've been talking only theory and words. These guys have been out doing it."

I know there were still some skeptics in the class, but our boldness to share the truth along with real-life examples seemed to embolden those timid souls who secretly believed but had previously been afraid and too intimidated to speak up.

The professor then surprised me as he addressed the class. "This has truly been our most fascinating class yet." He then turned to me and said with a subtle sadness and sense of regret, "I wish you had been my pastor when I was a kid." It seemed to me he was saying, "I am set in my place and position, and I don't see how I can change now, but if I had heard these things in my younger days, I might have taken a different road."

Certain principles were impressed upon my mind as I left that classroom. I saw very clearly the power of the truth and the reality of the Word of God and how it penetrates the heart when spoken with confidence that comes from the presence of the Holy Spirit who confirms it to the hearers.

I saw the blindness of the world and the emptiness of philosophy. Intellect can be impressive, but devoid of spiritual life, it is so empty. It does not touch the needs and hearts of the common man.

I also saw the weakness of silent, impotent Christians who do not speak up. That segment of the class had remained "invisible" when Nancy had been scorned for her belief. But upon hearing our message, they were emboldened to speak up.

I also saw the folly of mixture. Some of the students in that class believed some of the Bible but not all of it. Therefore, they had no real authority on which to base any argument or belief. To be selective with the Bible is to make yourself the authority. Therefore, you have no authority on which to base anything. When human reason is the final authority, we end up with millions of ideas and no real grounds or authority for any of it.

I have witnessed with my own eyes the reality of the Scripture. I have seen people healed through prayer. I have witnessed the miracle of a broken back healed instantly. I have witnessed a young man healed instantly of severe and advanced cases of asthma and emphysema as he was prayed for. I have cast demons out of people and witnessed the same effects as those described in the New Testament.

When given a chance, the Bible will come alive and prove itself true. I, therefore, choose to believe Moses, the apostles, and those saints who have given the Bible to us. I prefer to believe the written account of those eyewitnesses who walked with Jesus rather than putting my life and trust into the hands of modern, unbelieving philosophers who speak out of their own intellectual arrogance and emptiness.

> *[We have]... so great a salvation, which at the first began to be spoken by the Lord, and was confirmed to us by those who heard Him, God also bearing witness both with signs and wonders, with various miracles, and gifts of the Holy Spirit...*
>
> —HEBREWS 2:3B, 4A

> *And with great power the apostles gave witness to the resurrection of the Lord Jesus...*
>
> —ACTS 4:33

> *For we did not follow cunningly devised fables when we made known to you the power and coming of our Lord Jesus Christ, but were eyewitnesses of His majesty. For He received from God the Father honor and glory when*

*such a voice came to Him from the Excellent glory:
"This is My beloved Son, in whom I am well pleased."
And we heard this voice which came from heaven when
we were with Him on the holy mountain. And so we
have the prophetic word confirmed, which you do well
to take heed as a light shining in a dark place, until the
day dawns and the morning star rises in your hearts;
knowing this first, that no prophecy of Scripture is of
any private interpretation, for prophecy never came by
the will of man, but holy men of God spoke as they were
moved by the Holy Spirit.*

—2 PETER 1:16-21

10

MIRACLE AT THE YOUTH RETREAT: ROB'S HEALING

...And we are His witness to these things, and so also is the Holy Spirit whom God has given to those who obey Him.

— ACTS 5:32

W e usually think in terms of the Lord enabling us to share the good news of Jesus' death and resurrection, but we should not overlook the "also" in the verse quoted above. We should remember that He will walk beside us to give His own witness and add power to our testimony. We bear witness, but so does He. Below is a dramatic example of this second dimension of our testimony.

HIGH SCHOOL KIDS EXPERIENCE JESUS

In 1971, when Laurel and I were first married, we were asked to speak at a youth retreat for a group of high school kids from a Baptist church in Tulsa, Oklahoma. The youth pastor had prepared for the event by calling friends and intercessors to pray and fast for the Lord to visit these kids. There were about 40 of them at the event. Most of them attended church, but I don't think many of them really knew the Lord or had a real, personal relationship with Him.

Laurel sang, and I spoke. While I was sharing our testimony of our walk and experiences with the Lord, you could have heard a pin drop. It was as if Jesus was walking among us. His presence became more real each time I mentioned His name. A couple of the kids expressed a desire to know Him. Then, a few more. Suddenly, 20 of them were on their feet and praying with and for one another. The other 20, along with the football players, remained seated and just gazed in wonder at what was happening.

ROB'S HEALING

Then, a young man named Rob came up to me. He had both emphysema and asthma. His breathing was a loud wheezing and was so labored that it could be heard all over the room. He had a breathing machine with him, and his doctors had recommended that he not go to this retreat. But there he stood before me with a look of despair and desperation. I pulled him off to the side and said, "Rob, do you want to know Jesus?"

He said, "Yes," but then pointed to his chest to communicate the agony he was going through with his lungs.

I quoted Jesus' words about laying hands on the sick and then laid my hands on his head, asking Jesus to touch him.

Suddenly, he fell back and began to shout, "I can breathe! I can breathe!" The Lord had instantly healed him of the emphysema and asthma.

I then yelled out to the group, "Hey, Everybody... God just healed Rob!" Immediately, the other 20 kids rose up like a covey of quail. All 40 kids were standing with arms uplifted to the Lord, praising and thanking Him for the miracle. They all instantly gave their lives to the Lord and stood there weeping, laughing, and praising Him.

THE HOLY SPIRIT CONFIRMS OUR TESTIMONY

I did not orchestrate this. This event seemed so spontaneous; I simply watched it happen. I had told the group that Jesus died for our sins, had risen from the dead, and was alive now as living Lord and Savior. But as I was speaking, Jesus Himself was moving around that room apart from me and was speaking to them by the Holy Spirit. Their lives were transformed because God revealed Himself to them.

We speak of faith and of the need to believe, but there was in those days a dimension of God's presence that arose from sovereign acts of divine grace, providence, and purpose that transcended what we wanted. We did not cause it to happen. We simply responded to His presence. We testified, but He also testified.

May we, in this day, again proclaim the presence of Jesus, expecting that God will again "also bear witness both with signs and wonders, with various miracles and gifts of the Holy Spirit according to His own will" (Heb. 2:4).

> ...And we are His witness to these things, and so also is the Holy Spirit whom God has given to those who obey Him. (Acts 5:32)

> When the helper comes, whom I will send to you from the Father, the Spirit of truth who proceeds from the Father, He will testify of me. And you also will bear witness... (John 15:26-27)

A REUNION WITH ROB, 45 YEARS LATER

Following the retreat, the youth pastor invited me to meet with the group a couple of times and to teach them about the Holy

Spirit. This was my senior year at college. After I graduated from college, Laurel and I moved away and had not been in contact with Rob for the past 45 years. However, we often spoke of Rob and wondered where he was and how he was doing, and we often told the story of his healing. Then, recently, to my great surprise and delight, I received the following message on Facebook. Here is how the exchange went:

> ROB MITCHELL: Can you remember a youth retreat in the summer of '71 in Oklahoma? Steve Stockley was the youth pastor from Oral Roberts University. Were you the guest speaker?
>
> BILLY LONG: Rob, how could I forget that!!!! Such a wonderful retreat! Are you the Rob who was healed?
>
> ROB MITCHELL: Wow! This is great! Do you remember praying for me? I was completely healed that day, forever changed my life, and the lives of many others. I pastored for 20 years, and told my testimony everywhere I went. I'm crying like a baby just thinking about it. So much to tell you. Will surely talk some more, I still think of you and Laurel often.

Rob and his wife have five, wonderful, on-fire Christian children, and they currently lead a ministry in the toughest part of Tulsa. What a wonderful and joyful blessing it was to me and Laurel to reestablish contact with Rob, and now 45 years later, to hear him confirm the healing that took place at that retreat, knowing that he has been serving and walking with the Lord faithfully all these years. I am rejoicing and am so grateful to the Lord for allowing me to reestablish contact and hear the continuing story of his testimony. Praise the Lord!

11

MIRACLES WITH CHILDREN

Then they brought little children to Him, that He might touch them... And He took them up in His arms, laid His hands on them, and blessed them.

—MARK 10:13A, 16

CLAIRE

Claire was eight years old. She had two problems that troubled her: an embarrassing problem of bedwetting and a wart that had been on the bottom of her foot for over a year. She had heard her brother Reuben's story about the doctor cutting a wart from his foot, and she did not want that. She determined in her heart that she would wait for Mahesh Chavda to visit to our church and let him pray for her.

Claire, along with our other children, had come to love and respect Mahesh. They had heard him tell stories of the many healings that had taken place through his ministry around the world. And we had friends who had experienced healings in his meetings. Therefore, little eight-year-old Claire decided that Jesus would heal her when Mahesh came to minister.

She entered the meeting with a child's faith. She went up for prayer, and the Lord touched her. She was filled with the Holy

Spirit, the wart disappeared overnight and was completely gone the next morning, and she never wet the bed again.

LEAH

Leah was seven years old. She was trying to go to sleep but began to cry, saying, "Daddy and Mommy, my tummy hurts!" Laurel and I prayed for her, but the pain intensified, and she cried even harder. Finally, I turned to Laurel and said, "We need to take her to the emergency room."

Still in tears, Leah yelled out, "No! I don't want to go to the hospital. Pray for me. Jesus will heal me."

So, Laurel and I laid hands on her stomach and prayed in Jesus' name. The pain instantly and completely left. Leah suddenly became very calm and relaxed.

I leaned over and kissed her and said, "Leah, wasn't that nice of Jesus to touch you and take the pain away?"

She, with eyes half closed and ready now for sleep, peacefully and quietly said, "Yeah, cause if He didn't, He would be in trouble." I laughed under my breath and marveled at the simple faith of a child.

MATTHEW

Parents know how frightening it can be when their infant children get the croup. The croup is marked by episodes of harsh, hoarse, and dry coughing accompanied by difficult breathing. Our son, Matthew, was less than two years old and had developed a bad case of it. We were at a Bible study and prayer meeting at my parents' home. Matthew began to cough. His face turned red, and his breathing was difficult.

My cousin, Bootsie, said, "You need to take him to the emergency room." We considered this, but on the way home, faith rose in our hearts.

I turned to Laurel and said, "We are going to lay him in his crib and pray over him until he is healed." Upon entering the house, we laid him in the crib and prayed over him in Jesus' name. The Lord touched him, and he was healed the minute we began to pray. The cough was instantly and completely gone. He laid there quietly, consuming his bedtime formula, and fell into a restful sleep for the entire night. When he awoke the next morning, he had no symptoms at all. He was healed.

> *Let the little children come to me, and do not forbid them; for of such is the kingdom of God.*
>
> —MARK 10:14

12

WORD OF KNOWLEDGE: REVELATION REVEALS JESUS

...And thus the secrets of his heart are revealed; and falling down on his face, he will worship God and report that God is truly among you.

—1 CORINTHIANS 14:25

A LADY ON THE PLANE

On a flight to Raleigh, North Carolina, I was seated beside a lady who was flying into Columbia, South Carolina. As the plane was about to land in Columbia, I prayed quietly to myself, "Lord, this lady is about to get off the plane, and I have not said anything to her about You. Is there anything special I should say to her?"

Suddenly, the Holy Spirit gave me a name. (This is the only time this has ever happened to me.) I turned to her and said, "Who is Frank?"

Her expression froze, and she stared at me speechless with her mouth open.

I continued, "Sometimes, the Lord shows me things to pray for people, and I think the Lord has shown this to me for your sake. You can tell me. Who is Frank?"

She very sheepishly mumbled quietly, "Frank is a friend of mine who is having marriage problems."

I responded, "And Frank is coming to you for comfort... Isn't he?"

Still with her mouth open and staring at me in shock, she just shook her head and whispered, "Uh huh, yes, he is."

I then told her that the Lord loved her, had a plan for her, and wanted to reveal Himself to her, but the enemy had placed this temptation and stumbling block in her path to distract and lead her away. I encouraged her to go home and find a quiet place to sit and talk to God, to seek Him, and get to know Him.

Immediately, the plane was at the gate, and this lady got up and walked away still in a daze. I thought to myself, "She will go home with a fresh realization that there is a God who knows her and cares about her. Maybe she will look to heaven in faith and know that He is there and that He is listening to her."

A GENTLEMAN IN A RESTAURANT

I was having breakfast with a pastor friend of mine at a motel restaurant on Interstate 95 when I noticed a gentleman sitting alone at a table across the room. I turned to my friend and said, "Sam, you see that man over there? He is going through the pain of a divorce."

When Sam and I finished our breakfast, I noticed the gentleman was still at his table and decided to go to him. I walked over to his table and said to him, "Sir, my friend and I are pastors. When I saw you sitting here, the Lord showed me that you are going through the pain of a divorce, and I would like to pray for you."

The fellow stopped eating and looked up at me with sadness in his eyes. "I *am* in the middle of a divorce right now," he said.

I told him that the Lord loved him and wanted to deliver him from the things in his life that helped to cause the divorce. He responded, "I am from New England, and I am on my way now to Florida to get help for these very things."

I gave him my card and told him I would be praying for him.

About a week later, I received a letter from him in which he thanked me for reaching out to him. He shared how our meeting that morning had encouraged him. His faith was strengthened, and his hope was renewed because he was made aware that there really is a God who knows him and cares about him.

CONCLUSION

The purpose of the supernatural in the Church is not for show or theatrics. It is simply the presence of God at work. It happens when the people of God are moved with compassion and allow the Holy Spirit to work through them to encourage, strengthen, heal, comfort, and touch the people around them. God speaks and acts to reveal Himself.

> *...for the Lord revealed Himself to Samuel in Shiloh by the word of the LORD.*
>
> —1 SAMUEL 3:21B

13

"My Preacher is so Anointed He Pure Foams at the Mouth"

How do we expect people to act when they are being used by the Holy Spirit? A fellow once said to me, "My preacher is so anointed he pure foams at the mouth." That is a strange one, and I am thankful that the Lord does not expect us to do that. So what style should we use in our presentation?

A Spirit-filled Harvard professor very calmly walked up to someone and, in a very dignified and stolid voice, said, "This is what the Lord is saying to you: 'Your canines will develop acariases and become acaudal.'"

A backwoods farmer then walked up to the same person and, in a very emotional and energetic manner, said, "Thus saith the Lord: 'Thy dogs-uh will become infested with mites and lose their tails-uh.'"

The fact is these men said the exact same thing, but each one spoke out of his own personality and style. The Lord's Word was in the content while the style represented the individual vessel.

I want to share three examples below that show us we can be ourselves and not have to act a certain, expected way when we are being used by the Holy Spirit.

A *CASUAL* WORD THAT WAS SUPERNATURAL

I was visiting a church in Lexington, Kentucky a few years ago. The morning worship service had ended, and people were standing around the auditorium, talking and enjoying the fellowship of friends and family. I happened to notice two girls standing on the other side of the auditorium. I was acquainted with one of these girls from a singles conference at which I had recently spoken. I knew that this young lady would one day make some man a good wife, so I decided to walk over and, in a lighthearted and humorous way, encourage her.

I crossed the auditorium and went up to these two young ladies. As they turned to me, I said, "There is a crazy man out there!"

They both reacted with surprise and said, "What?"

I responded by addressing the unmarried girl with these words: "You are going to make some man a fine wife, and there is a crazy man out there for not having already snatched you up and married you!"

I was expecting her to respond with a laugh, but instead, her eyes filled with tears. I said, "What's wrong? What did I say to make her cry?"

Her friend then explained to me the conversation they were having just before I walked up. The single girl was sad because her fiancé had recently broken off their engagement. She was depressed and questioning herself, wondering why he had "dumped" her. As they stood there, she asked her friend, "Is something wrong with me that he would not want to marry me?"

The friend had responded, "No. There is nothing wrong with you. He's crazy!"

Then, "out of the blue" and totally unaware of the situation and their conversation, I walked up and said, "There is a crazy man out there."

I believed I was sent to encourage her. However, I was completely unaware of the significance of what I was saying until the friend explained to me how my words confirmed what she had said just moments before.

I was simply trying to encourage someone based on what I had seen with my natural eyes. I was not trying to be *spiritual* or do anything special. The timing, however, made the word supernatural.

A *SHORT* WORD THAT WAS SUPERNATURAL

During our first year of marriage, Laurel and I were part of a church in southern California. It was composed mostly of young people and had sprung up during the Jesus Movement and the outpouring of the Holy Spirit that was taking place at that time. Multitudes of kids were coming to know the living reality of Jesus Christ and His presence through the working of the Holy Spirit.

One thing that stands out in my memory of those days is the hunger for God that was demonstrated in the lives of those kids. They took their Bibles with them almost everywhere, they always had pen and paper to take notes during Bible study, and they all wanted to be used by God in some way.

In preparation for teaching a Bible study to a group of about 20 or 30 of these kids, I silently asked the Lord to confirm my direction for the teaching that night. Then, one of the boys stood up. I knew he was about to share what he thought would be a prophetic word from the Lord. He said, "The Lord wants us to watch and pray." He then paused and stood there silent for a minute, hoping to add something more significant. But that was it. He had nothing else to say, and so he sat down dejected and a little embarrassed, thinking he had failed.

I then stood up and said,

> Our friend has just given a short, simple word, telling us to watch and pray. He does not realize how the Lord has just used him. He has not only shared a word to which we should all take heed,

but also, without knowing it, he has given a word of confirmation to me. I was just now asking the Lord to confirm the teaching I am about to give. My text for tonight is Matthew 26:41, "Watch and pray..." My Bible was opened to that verse, and my eyes were on those very words as our friend was saying, "The Lord wants us to watch and pray."

A MIRACLE OF HEALING IN RESPONSE TO HARDLY A PRAYER

As I was leaving a friend's house one day, he and I passed his five-year-old son as he was playing with some toys on the ground. As we discussed other things, the father showed me some sort of bone growth that was on the back of the child's head. It was just a little smaller than half a ping-pong ball and had been there for years. The doctors had told him it was nothing to worry about. It would not harm the boy but was simply unattractive and inconvenient. My friend and I did not focus on the child but continued our conversation.

However, as I talked with my friend, I very casually laid my hand on the back of the child's head a couple of times, saying, "Lord, bless him." Again, I said, "I know it's nothing to worry about, but Lord, bless him anyway," as my friend and I went on with the conversation about other things. Then, I drove away, feeling guilty that I had not taken time to pray an official and "real" prayer over that child. Instead, I had only said, "Lord, bless him" in passing as I talked about other things.

I was surprised a couple of days later when my friend called to tell me that the child's growth had completely disappeared. The Lord had healed it in response to a simple, "bless-him" prayer.

SO, WHAT IS THE LESSON HERE?

While there are often unusual and strange occurrences during great visitations of God's presence, it is important for us to know that, generally speaking, we can move in the supernatural presence of the Holy Spirit in the normal, conversational tone of everyday life. How else can we approach the average person in the world with the reality of Jesus Christ? We can be ourselves. We don't have to act strange or change our voice. This is one of the keys to moving in the Holy Spirit on the job, in school, on the street, and out in the marketplace. You don't have to walk up to people and shout. You don't have to say "God-uh", "yea, yea", or "thus saith the Lord." You can be emotional or non-emotional. You can be enthusiastically zealous, or you can be quiet and reserved. The key is to be genuine and real.

The supernatural is not what you do but rather what God Himself does. Sometimes, God's work is seen as obviously and patently supernatural. Other times, it can be hidden and unnoticed because it is defined by the context and timing and may be significant only to those to whom it is directed.

When we care about people and reach out to them in a real and genuine manner, we will see God at work. And, as in the examples given above, we may find out later that He was at work when we were not aware of it. We may be able to say as Jacob did, "Surely the Lord is in this place, and I did not know it" (Gen. 28:16b).

14

PUFF AND BLUFF

There are three erroneous approaches to the subject of Satan and demons. The first is the open and active involvement in demonic activity as in the occult, psychic phenomena, and the animism of primitive societies. The second erroneous approach is to deny their existence altogether. The third and somewhat irrational approach is that of Christians who believe in the existence of evil spirits because they read about them in the Bible but simply ignore the subject as if the evil spirits described in the biblical examples somehow mysteriously faded into the background and do not relate in any real way to our contemporary society except to entice people to sin.

The spiritual realm as described in the Bible is real. If we will follow the biblical pattern, we will present the subject of the demonic in a balanced and proper perspective. But still, it is difficult to make it palatable to those who reject the Bible or the reality of the spiritual realm.

THE PUFF ADDER

When I was a young child, I came upon a snake that frightened me. It coiled up, looked right at me with its head raised, and puffed up, making a hissing noise. I started to back away, but a friend told me not to fear because this was merely a puff adder. It had no venom and could do no harm but was simply putting on a show to intimidate me. I picked up a stick and poked gently in the snake's face. The snake then employed a new scheme when it realized its strategy had failed. It flipped over, belly up, and pretended to be dead with its mouth disjointed and tongue hanging out to the side as if it had been beaten to death. I took the stick and tried a few times to turn the snake back over to its normal position. But it wanted me to think it was dead, so it kept flipping itself back over onto the belly-up position. Its fierceness was only a bluff.

THE GIRL WITH A DEMON

A young girl was involved with a fellow who practiced Satan worship. She had decided to leave home and run away with him. One of her friends, however, brought her to Laurel and me, hoping we could persuade the girl to change her mind.

As we sat in our living room, I addressed the girl with these words:

> We are living in a day in which there is much spiritual activity. God is pouring out His Holy Spirit, and we are witnessing a visitation of God's presence and a revival in the gifts of the Holy Spirit and the supernatural presence of Jesus Christ in His Church. But there is also intensification in the realm of darkness which is trying to counterfeit the working of the Holy Spirit. This counterfeit is seen in the surge of demonic activity in the areas of psychic, occult, and New Age activity.

I proceeded to tell the young lady that this rise in spiritual stirrings had created a great hunger in the youth of her generation and that she was faced with a choice. She could turn to the Lord and experience the treasures He is making available, or she could follow her boyfriend in Satan worship and enter the bondage and deception of demonic activity.

At that point in the conversation, an unusual thing began to occur unexpectedly. As I spoke to her, she began to twitch and tremble, and her eyes began to turn up in their sockets. Laurel and I looked at each other, knowing that the Lord's presence had stirred up a demon in the girl. I then told the girl,

> What you are experiencing right now is an evil spirit that entered you as a result of your involvement with your boyfriend in Satan-worship. We are going to cast it out.

The girl immediately held up both hands with clenched fists and, with a very angry and threatening expression on her face, said, "Don't bother me. There is no telling what I might do!"

I was surprised by this unexpected response. As I paused for a second, Laurel immediately spoke to the spirit, saying, "We are not afraid of you. Come out of this girl now!"

The threatening and intimidating expression on the girl's face immediately changed from anger to fear and grief. She began to cry as she actually slithered out of the chair and onto the floor. The demon came out of her with groans and cries.

The spirit in the girl behaved in a similar fashion to that of the puff adder snake. It first tried to intimidate and frighten. But it came out of the girl when faced with the reality of Jesus' presence and our knowledge of the authority we have in His name.

A SUPERSTITIOUS COUPLE

A few years ago, I was talking with a husband and wife who were beginning to delve into witchcraft and thought they had received communications from dead relatives. I shared the gospel with them, pointing them to Jesus and telling them that the Bible forbids involvement in these occult activities because witchcraft is of the devil, and ghosts are not dead people but are, in fact, demons or evil spirits pretending to be dead people.

The enemy was angry that I had shared the truth of the gospel with this couple.

Later on that day, I was in my motel room, working at my computer when, all of a sudden, a couple of cans of tuna sitting on the microwave were thrown across the room and onto the floor. It was a spirit trying to frighten me and intimidate me into not sharing the gospel with this couple.

I was not afraid but felt the power of the Holy Spirit and the righteous indignation of the Lord rise up within me. I immediately stood to my feet and commanded the spirit to depart, leave, and not come back.

I immediately felt the peace and joy of the Holy Spirit. I took a few minutes to praise the Lord for the truth of His Word, for the efficacy of the blood of Jesus, and for the power and joy of His presence. I then went back to my computer and finished my work.

THE BLUFF

Bluff means "to deter or frighten by pretense or a mere show of strength; to deceive an opponent in cards by a bold bet on an inferior hand with the result that the opponent withdraws a winning hand." This is how the devil operates. He seeks to frighten and intimidate us. This strategy often works on believers who do not know the Scripture, the power of God, and their authority in Jesus' name.

As believers, we need not fear. Christ has delivered us from the kingdom of darkness and transferred us into His kingdom. He defeated Satan at Calvary and stripped him of his power.

Satan can only rule over those who choose to serve him and follow him and his ways. To gain advantage and control over

Christians, he must use fear, discouragement, deception, accusation, and enticements to sin. Fear and discouragement lead to unbelief and disobedience. Deception leads people astray into error, accusation produces guilt which hinders faith and confidence, and sin causes people to turn away from God.

But when confronted head-on and in the open, the enemy tries to bluff his way by appearing strong and threatening. But he knows he is defeated. He knows that we, as followers of Jesus, are victorious in our God. The main point I want to emphasize is that we need to know it.

ONE OF OUR WEAPONS

The authority and power to cast out demons is part of the arsenal of tools Jesus has given to the Church. But sadly, exorcism is one area of ministry that often is either neglected and misunderstood or abused and carried to extremes. Every church leader and minister should be trained in exorcism. Every follower of Jesus who is filled with the Holy Spirit and instructed in the biblical and wise approach to the subject can experience the presence of God in seeing people delivered from the oppression of evil spirits.

> *Then the seventy returned with joy saying, "Lord, even the demons are subject to us in Your name." And He said to them, "I saw Satan fall like lightning from heaven. Behold, I give you authority… over all the power of the enemy, and nothing shall by any means hurt you. Nevertheless, do not rejoice in this, that the spirits are subject to you, but rather rejoice because your names are written in heaven."*

> —LUKE 10:17-20

Philip went down to the city of Samaria and preached Christ to them. And the multitudes with one accord heeded the things spoken by Philip, hearing and seeing the miracles which he did. For unclean spirits, crying with a loud voice, came out of many... and many who were paralyzed and lame were healed. And there was great joy in that city.

—ACTS 8:5-8

15

HOLDING FAST THE GOOD

If a cat sits on a hot stove, he will never sit on a hot stove again. But by the same token, he will never sit on a cold one either.

—MARK TWAIN

We fail to see the beauty and good purpose of a thing when blinded by prejudice, bias, and misinformation. Bad experiences often cause us to avoid even the good ones. Therefore, I am reaching out to those who have never done a biblical study of the Holy Spirit's work and to those who have been "turned off" by bad examples. I encourage you to take another look at the subject from a biblical perspective rather than taking cues from negative experiences that may have obscured the actual biblical model—that is, the way they did it in the New Testament Church.

Don't stumble over bad examples.

> Do not quench the Spirit. Do not despise prophecies. Test all things; hold fast what is good. (1 Thess. 5:19-21)

I have witnessed miracles and been a part of miracles. I have known His power and believe in God and His desire to work intimately in the lives of people. But then, I also have experienced times when I was in "the deep" and about to be swallowed up and close to losing everything. Knowing of my failures and struggles, one might then say, "Where is your God?" We don't have all the answers. We don't always do everything right. We make mistakes, and we stumble, but because of our hunger to know God and His intimate presence, we step out in faith, trust Him to teach us, and we press on to grow in the things of the Spirit.

I could tell you of friends who have been healed through prayer and also of others dying in spite of it. I have friends who have experienced miraculous healings and friends who have been raised from the dead. Some have received an immediate response to prayer, and others have suffered what seems an interminable wait as they call on the Lord daily for healing, help, or an "open door." My experiences, however, do not change the truth. My success or failure does not change the reality of God's Word and the work of Holy Spirit.

It is arrogant to think that something is not real simply because I have not done it or seen it. One man boasted that miracles were not real today because not one miracle had ever occurred in any church in his denomination. That statement is no basis for a theology that denies miracles. It is, however, an indictment against his denomination.

The New Testament Church knew both the reality of a sovereign God and the reality of human weakness. They were not afraid of God's presence, and they were not daunted by human weakness and propensity toward mistakes. The first apostles did not prohibit the supernatural working of the Holy Spirit when they saw abuses and misuses. Instead, they provided instruction and wisdom. They threw out the bad apples but ate the good ones. They did not quench or despise the working of the Holy Spirit but proved all things and *held fast the good.*

IF YOU AVOID ALL EGGS, YOU'LL NEVER EAT A ROTTEN ONE

We should not use "bad apples" as an excuse to avoid all "apples." Grocery stores and trees are full of good apples, and it is extremely rare to find a bad one. When I was a kid, I found a worm in a peach taken from a tree in our yard, but it did not stop me from eating peaches. I found a rotten egg once when I was a child. It stank worse than anything I had ever smelled before or since. But I knew that it was an exception to the norm. Eggs are good, so I continue to enjoy them as a part of my usual breakfast menu. I did not let one bad egg cause me henceforth to approach all eggs cautiously as if they might be rotten.

If you were to visit a church where people were swinging from the chandeliers or behaving strangely, would you then reject emotions and joy in your spiritual walk? Would you say, "These people are crazy", and use this as an excuse to avoid any search for God? Or would you search for the reasonable, biblical pattern for worship and the healthy expression of joy and emotions? Would you read the Bible to find out what it really says or just assume that the "apple" or "egg" you found represented the norm for all "apples" and "eggs"?

The things people usually fear in spiritual experiences are not the true biblical patterns but rather the unreal "phantoms" they have created in their own minds as a result of prejudiced propaganda or experiences with bad examples, which most likely were exaggerations or soulish aberrations of the true biblical model. For example, I have seen and heard some preachers who caused me to flinch, but the greatest portion of my experience has been with the many stable, sincere, and gifted men of God who serve the Lord faithfully and wisely. The preachers we see portrayed on the typical TV show and in the movies are usually parodies or burlesque exaggerations of the real thing. Anyone investigating a spiritual truth or experience should go to the Bible first and see what is actually described there, rather than skipping the biblical model and arguing against the distorted, the false, or the counterfeit they may have encountered. Our hunger to know God should cause us to wade past the stumbling blocks, go to His Word, call out to Him, and search for the real thing.

This principle is especially true in the matter of the supernatural manifestation of God's presence among His people. The problem is that people tend to approach the gifts and manifestations of the Holy Spirit initially from a negative perspective. Rather than welcoming the potential of God's wonderful presence supernaturally at work among us, they begin with a negative disposition, seeing the working of the Holy Spirit as a necessary evil and something from which to protect themselves. Their first response is not to hunger for the amazing, positive possibilities but rather to assume a defensive posture with their primary focus on avoiding the abuses. They are so worried about the "bathwater" that they don't see the baby. The result is avoidance, severe regulation, or prohibition. We should not fear the presence of God. Jesus, in referring to the Holy Spirit, said,

> If a son asks for bread from any father among you, will he give him a stone? Or if he asks for a fish, will he give him a serpent instead of a fish? Or if he asks for an egg, will he offer him a scorpion? If you... know how to give good gifts to your children, how much more will your heavenly Father give the Holy Spirit to those who ask Him. (Luke 11:11-13)

To always expect the "scorpion" rather than the "egg" is an expression of unbelief and is a lack of confidence in God's goodness and in His ability to manage His Church.

This tendency to approach God's presence negatively with fear causes churches and Christians to remain in "safe" waters where the boat will not be rocked and where there is no need for discernment or risk-taking. We don't have to worry about the "bathwater" problem if we don't have the "baby" among us. We don't have to worry about "cleaning the stall" if we don't have an "ox" in the barn. We don't have to worry about a "rotten egg" if we just avoid all eggs. This fear causes us to miss out on the adventures of life. It keeps us from launching out into the deep and witnessing the supernatural presence of God at work.

The point here is that the Church should not be ruled by the fear of misuse and abuse of spiritual things. The Church should be secure and discerning enough to move out courageously and in faith into the wonderful area of God's presence at work among us, not fearing the awkwardness and stumbles that are often necessary in the growth and learning process. We see this principle in the example of how Jesus trained the 12 disciples. He knew the mistakes they would make, but He did not "roll His eyes" and withdraw. Instead, He "rolled up his sleeves" and moved on with the full training program. We should follow His example.

> *Do not quench the Spirit. Do not despise prophecies.*
> *Test all things; hold fast that which is good.*

> —1 THESSALONIANS 5:9-21

16

SPIRITUAL GIFTS AND GODLY CHARACTER

And though I have the gift of prophecy, and understand all mysteries and all knowledge, and though I have all faith, so that I could remove mountains, but have not love, I am nothing.

—1 CORINTHIANS 13:2

Knowledge puffs up, but love edifies.

—1 CORINTHIANS 8:1B

Many will say to me in that day, "Lord, Lord, have we not prophesied in Your name, cast out demons in Your name, and done many wonders in Your name?" And then I will declare to them, "I never knew you; depart from Me, you who practice lawlessness!"

—MATTHEW 7:22, 23

Truth must be accompanied by compassion, godly character, and integrity. This principle applies to any aspect of our relationship with the Lord and His Word whether it be Bible study, preaching, personal counsel, exhortation, or prophecy. Complications arise when the "carnal" man—rather than the spiritual man—handles the Word of God. The lack of compassion causes it to be used as a legalistic hammer to condemn and hurt people. The lack of character and holiness brings deception, mixture, and contamination. The lack of integrity causes men to "use" people and act with wrong and selfish motives.

When we think of spiritual gifts, we think of God's power. But God's power must not be divorced from godly character and God's holiness. Good character and integrity are the things that prevent prophecy and the other gifts from being "flash" and glitter. Character is the foundation for the anointing and a ministry that has purity and durability. A person's bad character can destroy what his or her gift builds. It is essentially character, not gifting, that determines whether or not we pass the tests of life.

Therefore, we seek to walk in God's holiness as well as in His power. Power without holiness and character is empty and rings hollow. The world will scorn us if we walk in the power of God but fail in the holiness of God. The holiness of God—that is, right living, right motives, and moral purity—is what distinguishes us from the rest of the world. The devil can imitate our noise and power, but he cannot reproduce holiness and godly character. The devil's counterfeit imitation of God's power is seen in soulish mysticism, sorcery, witchcraft, the occult, and psychic phenomena. His attempts at imitating holiness and character become legalism and bondage.

Godly character is something we, as Christians, must be careful to cultivate. Good people excelling at good things have to beware of pride. Immature and unlearned people must remain humble in order to learn and avoid the paths of error. People who experience the power and working of the Holy Spirit must especially guard their hearts to maintain integrity and pure motives.

There have been men and women of God who moved in healing and power gifts yet fell because they were deceived into thinking God was overlooking their sin. Because the miracles continued and because God was still using them, they presumed to think God was giving them special dispensation to continue in their sin with impunity.

The fact is the Holy Spirit will continue to use a person who is in disobedience and sin, at least for a season, while the Holy Spirit tries to draw him to repentance in the particular area of transgression. However, eventually, "the bottom will drop out," and the person will face the consequences of his or her unrepentant sin. Sometimes, the problem may be related to an area of stubbornness, an area which grieves the Lord. Whether sin or childish stubbornness, a person eventually may face either judgment or discipline.

In this same vein of thought, it should be noted that some very interesting—though, not godly—people have prophesied. Balaam was a soothsayer who spoke some wonderful prophetic words over Israel, words that even prophesied of Jesus (Num. 22-23). King Saul prophesied even while trying find and kill David (1 Sam. 10:6, 12; 19:24). The high priest Caiaphas, while leading the plot to put Jesus to death, prophesied that one must die for the nation (John 11:51). These examples—along with some you know of personally—show us that the gifts and manifestations of the Holy Spirit operate by the mercy and grace of God and that God will use imperfect vessels.

The imperfections may be related to ungodly character—like those discussed above—or to issues related to normal spiritual growth and character development experienced by all Christians. If the issues relate to sin and evil, we should repent and change. If the issues relate to the stumbles and imperfections of normal growth, we should recognize that mistakes are a part of growth, be thankful for the disciplines of learning, and move forward, rejoicing in the grace, mercy, and goodness of the Lord.

Part 2

PROPHETIC MINISTRY

17

INTRODUCTION TO PROPHETIC MINISTRY

The prophetic ministry, as portrayed in the New Testament Church, is either unknown or greatly misunderstood by too many Christians today. When the term, *prophesying*, is mentioned, most people think of the Old Testament prophets, biblical end-time prophecies, or psychic phenomena (the demonic counterfeit of the true spiritual gift taught in Scripture).

In this section, I want to show how the prophetic ministry operated among the first Christians as recorded in the New Testament. Their practice should be the model that we emulate in our Christian walk today. We should do what they did.

MY FIRST EXPERIENCES WITH PROPHETIC MINISTRY

The gifts and manifestations of the Holy Spirit came alive to me when I received the baptism in the Holy Spirit in 1967 during the outpouring of the Holy Spirit that became known as the Charismatic Renewal. It was not uncommon to hear people giving general prophetic words to congregations or to the people gathered for worship. At some point in the meeting, a person might stand up and give a brief prophetic message, often beginning with the phrase, "Thus says the Lord." I learned later that a prophetic word does not have to begin with that phrase. I learned that these prophetic messages often are given to individuals as well as to groups and can be spoken in a more casual rather than religious style.

The first time I witnessed the prophetic ministry in which supernatural words were given to individuals was when my wife, Laurel, and I visited in the home of Leland Davis. Our testimony had been published in the Oral Roberts Evangelistic Association's *Abundant Life Magazine*; unsurprisingly, I had in my possession a rather large stack of these magazines that I kept on hand to pass out to people. When Laurel and I arrived at Leland Davis' house, one of the first things I did was to hand him a copy. I guess I thought he would be impressed.

After the evening meal, we went with him to church where he was the guest minister that night. After his sermon, he began to move in his prophetic gifting, going from one individual to another, giving very encouraging supernatural words. This was the first time I had seen the prophetic ministry at this depth.

My jaw dropped, and, with mouth open, I realized what a novice I was. I was ready to ask Leland to give back my magazine. I had given it to him with such an air of youthful arrogance. Now, I was humbled into realizing there is more… more to learn, more to experience, and more to grow into.

It is such arrogance for us to think we "have arrived" and that we are so "deep," thus losing our hunger to grow and reach forward. If we look back in awe at how far we have come, we should look forward and be humbled by how far there is yet to go.

A GENERAL INTRODUCTION TO PROPHECY

In the New Testament Church, *prophecy* is not "preaching." Prophecy is speaking by immediate revelation and by inspiration of the Holy Spirit. It can relate to the past, present, or future. The time aspect is not primary; rather, it is the Lord's speaking to encourage, comfort, strengthen, or to bring some revelation.

Prophecy is the Holy Spirit moving upon one to speak a word from God to a specific person or people. It can appear amazingly supernatural, or it can sound very simple and uneventful to those standing by. It can be an intense and dramatic word or a quiet and gentle word to remind someone that God loves him or her. It is not to be confused with or equated with psychic phenomena, which are demonic counterfeits of the spiritual gifts listed in 1 Corinthians 12.

A careful reading of the New Testament reveals three levels of prophecy operating in the early Christian Church.

1. The office of a prophet (Eph. 4:11; Acts 21:10-12)
2. The ministry of prophecy in which a person is specially gifted in ministering to others prophetically (Rom. 12:6; Acts 21:9)
3. The manifestation of the Holy Spirit ("You can all prophesy," 1 Cor. 14: 24, 31)

Here are some examples in Scripture that establish the fact that the prophetic ministry existed in the New Testament Church as a manifestation of the Holy Spirit:

> But the manifestation of the Spirit is given to each one for the profit of all... to another prophecy... (1 Cor. 12:7a, 10b)

> Pursue love, and desire spiritual gifts, but especially that you may prophesy. (1 Cor. 14:1)

> Now his father Zacharias was filled with the Holy Spirit, and prophesied... (Luke 1:67)

> And in these days prophets came from Jerusalem to Antioch. Then one of them, named Agabus,

stood up and showed by the Spirit that there was going to be a great famine throughout all the world, which also happened in the days of Claudius Caesar. (Acts 11:27-28)

Now in the church that was at Antioch there were certain prophets and teachers: Barnabas, Simeon who was called Niger, Lucius of Cyrene, Manaen who had been brought up with Herod the tetrarch, and Saul. As they ministered to the Lord and fasted, the Holy Spirit said, "Now separate to Me Barnabas and Saul for the work to which I have called them." (Acts 13:1-2)

...the Holy Spirit testifies in every city, saying that chains and tribulations await me. (Acts 20:23b)

Now this man had four daughters who prophesied. (Acts 21:9)

...a certain prophet named Agabus came down from Judea. When he had come to us, he took Paul's belt, bound his own hands and feet, and said, "Thus says the Holy Spirit, 'So shall the Jews at Jerusalem bind the man who owns this belt, and deliver him into the hands of the Gentiles.'" (Acts 21:10b-11)

This charge I commit to you, son Timothy, according to the prophecies previously made concerning you, that by them you may war the good warfare. (1 Tim. 1:18)

Do not neglect the gift that is in you, which was
given to you by prophecy with the laying on of the
hands of the eldership. (1 Tim. 4:14)

The verses listed above should convince the open-minded
reader to acknowledge that the New Testament Christians
experienced something more than we customarily see in our
typical worship service and Christian fellowship. Prophecy and
the other gifts of the Spirit are meant to be instruments of
compassion in which the Lord works through us to encourage
and strengthen one another.

18

PROPHECY CONFIRMS AND ENCOURAGES

This chapter begins a series of 4 parts that deal with the purpose of the prophetic ministry in the New Testament Church.

THE SETTING

At this point, it is important to help you envision what the prophetic ministry looks like in the New Testament Church.

A prophetic word can come through one who functions in the office of a prophet and proclaims what God is saying to a church, a group of people, a nation, or the world (Eph. 4:11; Acts 21:10-12). It can come through a church member who is not a prophet but who has a special gift to move in prophetic ministry as he or she reaches out to others (Rom. 12:6; Acts 21:9). It can also come as a manifestation of the Holy Spirit through any Spirit-filled believer as the Lord chooses to use him or her; the Bible says, "You can all prophesy" (see 1 Cor. 12:7, 10; 14:1-5, 24, 31).

Prophecy is the Holy Spirit inspiring a person to speak a word from God's heart. It may be directed to a congregation or to an individual. The typical setting might be fellowship at church or Christians together in someone's living room. It can occur during worship or during casual fellowship over a cup of coffee.

It can be a simple statement made in normal conversation and as inconspicuous as the inspiration to tell someone the Lord loves him or her, or it can be as dramatic as the prophet Agabus picking up the Apostle Paul's belt and binding his own hands and feet, saying, "So shall the Jews at Jerusalem bind the man who owns this belt, and deliver him into the hands of the Gentiles" (Acts 21:11b).

Sometimes, a person is moved upon by the Holy Spirit to give a word to a church. Sometimes, he or she receives a special anointing to pray or share a thought in response to someone who has opened his or her heart or shared a need. Under a prophetic anointing, those prayers and words will speak directly to the situation, whether to a church or to an individual being prayed for and ministered to.

PROPHECY CONFIRMS

A young man named Tom came to me for counsel and discussed various issues he was dealing with in his life. I shared with him four or five major principles that applied to his situation. The next day, Leland Davis—a genuine New Testament prophet who had no knowledge of Tom's situation—was the guest speaker at our church. I stood amazed as he spoke over Tom a word of encouragement that contained in detail each of the points I had given in my counsel the night before. Tom was comforted by these words of confirmation and was able to be at peace.

PROPHECY "DIRECTS" BUT ONLY IN A LIMITED SENSE

A prophetic word will generally confirm rather than direct. A person receiving a prophetic word should not act on a "prophetic" word that gives direction "out of the blue." He should identify with the word and should have an inner witness that affirms its authenticity. If this assurance and peace is missing, he should either reject the word or place it in the "pending" file to be revisited later.

The prophetic word to the church in Acts 13:1-3 was not a strange word "out of the blue" but rather confirmed what had already been planned. The Spirit was telling them the time had arrived for them to commission Paul and Barnabas for the work to which they had already been called. The word confirmed the timing of the ministry.

In Acts 16:6-10, the Holy Spirit spoke strongly and emphatically to the apostolic team, forbidding them to go into Asia and not permitting them to go into Bithynia. This direction obviously came through a very strong inner sense of what God was saying and was almost certainly accompanied by prophetic words similar to those prophecies that warned Paul about his trip to Jerusalem (Acts 20:23). Following these words of caution and restriction, Paul received a positive direction through a vision in the night instructing him to go to Macedonia (Acts 16:9).

PROPHECY IS AN INSTRUMENT OF GOD'S LOVE IN REACHING OUT TO PEOPLE

> *Pursue love, and desire spiritual gifts, especially that you may prophesy.*
>
> —1 CORINTHIANS 14:1

The purpose of the supernatural in the Church is not for show or theatrics. It is simply the presence of God at work. It happens when the people of God are moved with compassion and allow the Holy Spirit to work through them to encourage, strengthen, heal, comfort, and touch the people around them. God speaks and acts to reveal Himself through our words, our prayers, or a compassionate touch on someone's shoulder.

PROPHECY IS MEANT TO BUILD UP AND ENCOURAGE.

> *He who prophesies speaks edification and exhortation and comfort to men… he who prophesies edifies the church.*
>
> —1 CORINTHIANS 14:3, 4B

> *But the manifestation of the Spirit is given to each one for the profit of all… to another prophecy…*
>
> —1 CORINTHIANS 14:12:7, 10

The prophetic word edifies or builds up those to whom it is directed. It strengthens and assists with growth. It also exhorts, which refers to words that motivate, prod, and urge us strongly toward obedience and faithfulness. It can be a word of comfort given to bring relief from suffering and grief. It can be a special word from the Lord to lighten the countenance, give courage, renew hope, and free one from despair and dismay.

AN EXAMPLE

I was speaking at a church in Florence, South Carolina one Sunday when the Lord gave me a prophetic word for a young man in the congregation. After having him stand, I told him, "You are about to experience a job change. But don't be afraid or dismayed. The Lord is in it."

When he went back to work that week, he was told his job was being eliminated. He was not discouraged or afraid. The Lord had prepared him through the word he had received. A better job opened up for him very quickly in Myrtle Beach, South Carolina.

A prophetic word confirms that God knows us, cares about us, and is involved intimately in our lives.

19

PROPHECY IS AN INSTRUMENT OF IMPARTATION AND REVELATION

A prophetic word may confront people with the truth about themselves. It convinces them that God is present and that He sees and knows.

> But if all prophesy, and an unbeliever or an uninformed person comes in, he is convinced by all, he is convicted by all. And thus the secrets of his heart are revealed; and so, falling down on his face, he will worship God and report that God is truly among you. (1 Cor. 14:24-25)

I was speaking at a church one evening when the Lord began to give me words for individuals. When receiving prophetic ministry, people will often weep when they realize the Lord really does know what they are going through and that He is reaching out to them in a special way to show His love and care. However, on this particular night, I saw a lady and some people get up and walk out. The pastor later told me they left the building because they were afraid I might minister to them. Maybe they had things to hide and were afraid I might expose them. Or, maybe they were simply unfamiliar and were afraid of the unknown. Nevertheless, I am absolutely confident that nothing would have been said to embarrass or make them uncomfortable. The Holy Spirit comes to express the same love and power that worked through Jesus when He spoke to and touched people during His earthly ministry.

While visiting in a home few years ago, I saw in the Spirit that one of the Christian men was struggling with a very serious temptation. I pulled him aside and ministered to him privately. I simply told him what the Lord had shown me, gave to him a word of caution, and then prayed that the Lord would deliver him.

Jesus' ministry to the woman at the well is a prime example of how prophetic insight, accompanied by a word of knowledge, can penetrate the heart and draw someone to the Lord. Jesus told her to call her husband to come to him.

She responded, "I have no husband."

Jesus then said, "You have well said, 'I have no husband,' for you have had five husbands, and the one whom you now have is not your husband" (John 4:17b, 18b).

The woman's life was changed. She went and shared her experience with the men of the city. "Come see a man who told me all things that I ever did. Could this be the Christ?" (John 4:29). As a result of her words, these men left the city and came to Jesus.

Prophecy may reveal knowledge and give spiritual instruction. Encouragement often comes with understanding.

> For you can all prophesy one by one, that all may
> learn and all may be encouraged. (1 Cor. 14:31)

Prophecy is not preaching or teaching, yet it may include words that enlighten and instruct. The seed of learning is always present when the Lord speaks to us.

Prophecy may show things to come or reveal what God is about to do.

> Surely the Lord GOD does nothing, unless He
> reveals His secret to His servants the prophets.
> (Amos 3:7)

> And in these days prophets came from Jerusalem
> to Antioch. Then one of them, named Agabus,
> stood up and showed by the Spirit that there was
> going to be a great famine throughout all the
> world, which also happened in the days of
> Claudius Caesar. (Acts 11:27-28)

> ...a certain prophet named Agabus came down
> from Judea. When he had come to us, he took
> Paul's belt, bound his own hands and feet, and
> said, "Thus says the Holy Spirit, so shall the Jews
> at Jerusalem bind the man who owns this belt, and
> deliver him into the hands of the Gentiles."
> (Acts 21:10b-11)

As I stated in a previous chapter, prophecy in the New
Testament Church is defined as speaking by immediate
revelation and by inspiration from the Holy Spirit. It can relate to
the past, present, or future. While it may speak about the future,
the time aspect is not primary. The primary aspect is that the Lord
is speaking to encourage, comfort, strengthen, or to bring some
revelation.

Prophecy is useful in the impartation of spiritual gifts and in
confirming and launching individuals into ministry.

> As they ministered to the Lord and fasted, the
> Holy Spirit said, "Now separate to Me Barnabas
> and Saul for the work to which I have called
> them." (Acts 13:2)

> Do not neglect the **gift** that is in you, which was

given to you by prophecy with the laying on of hands of the eldership. (1 Tim. 4:14)

The Holy Spirit spoke supernaturally through prophetic words when the Apostles Paul and Barnabas began their apostolic and missionary journeys. Timothy's ministry also began with the impartation of his ministry gift through the laying on of hands and prophetic words from Paul and church elders. The Old Testament shows Samuel prophetically confirming Saul's and David's call as Kings.

We often hear people speak of being "called" to their work or ministry. Usually, they "hear" this call in their own hearts in their relationship and walk with the Lord. But the Lord will also confirm that call through others in the Body of Christ. That confirmation may be a simple affirmation from others who agree, or it may be a strong prophetic word as noted in the verses quoted above.

20

Prophecy Strengthens Us for Spiritual Warfare

A prophetic word can impart faith and strength to stand during spiritual warfare and when encountering assaults against us, our faith, and our work.

> This charge I commit to you, son Timothy, according to the prophecies previously made concerning you, that by them you may wage the good warfare. (1 Tim. 1:18)

Timothy received prophetic words that confirmed his call and the specific work he was about to do. Those words were given through Paul, the elders, or other saints in the local church. According to Paul, these prophetic words would sustain and strengthen Timothy during the spiritual warfare he was certain to encounter. These prophecies would sustain him in the face of the struggles, persecutions, and tribulations that would come with advancing the Kingdom of God.

This principle of "waging a good warfare" or "fighting the good fight" through the prophetic word is also illustrated in the life of the Apostle Paul. A prophetic word can have the same effect as the instruction Jesus gave to Paul regarding his subsequent travel to Rome. The risen Lord appeared to Paul in the night and said, "...as you have testified for me at Jerusalem, so you must also bear witness at Rome" (Acts 23:11b). This word gave Paul the assurance that, whatever else might happen on the journey, it was inevitable that he would end up in Rome to preach the gospel there. This word sustained him as death threatened him many times on this particular journey.

More than 40 men banded together with an oath that they would not eat or drink until they killed him. I can imagine Paul thinking, "You men are going to be mighty hungry and thirsty because I am going to Rome."

He was held in chains by the Roman authorities while the Jewish leaders wanted him taken to Jerusalem where he could be put to death. Paul's response: "I am going to Rome" (Acts 23:12-14).

On a Roman ship in the Mediterranean Sea, a severe and violent storm threatened to destroy the ship and everyone on it. Paul said, "I'll not die here. I am going to Rome" (Acts 27:24).

When the ship ran aground and was breaking up, the soldiers were about to kill the prisoners, including Paul, but the centurion stopped them. Paul was "going to Rome" (Acts 27:2-3).

The passengers were marooned on the island of Malta. While gathering wood for a fire, Paul was bitten by a poisonous viper. Everyone watched, expecting him to fall over dead, but he shook off the snake and suffered no harm. He was "going to Rome" (Acts 28:4-5).

The prophetic ministry in Christian fellowship often works on the same principle. When the Lord speaks to confirm His plan or purpose or to encourage us in an endeavor, we can stand on that word. Of course, the Bible is the written and final Word of God on which we stand as the foundation for our faith and life in Christ. But the Holy Spirit does give us specific prophetic words, such as those given to Timothy, to encourage us and help us to "fight the good fight."

On one occasion when I faced a difficult decision, I told the Lord that I did not have the courage or strength in myself to do what He was calling me to do. I did not want to refuse or say "no" to God, so I went to the Lord with these words:

> My Lord, I do not want to make such a decision out of the imaginations of my own heart. The only way I can obey is to know that I have heard your voice, to know I have a clear commission from You. Only then will I be able to face the struggles and difficulties that might accompany this step.

This is why Peter, standing in the boat during the storm, said to Jesus, "Lord, if it is You, command me to come to you on the water" (Matt. 14:28b). Peter knew he would be able to take that step of faith only if he was certain Jesus was telling him to come. The same principle was at work when Peter responded to Jesus' instructions to cast his net into the water:

> Master, we have toiled all night and caught nothing. Nevertheless, at your word I will let down the net. (Luke 5:5)

Of course, the Lord can and does speak to us personally and directly by the Holy Spirit in our daily walk with Him as we pray and read our Bibles. But He will not allow us to be so independent that we get everything we need from Him without receiving from others. He delights in Christians blessing and serving one another. We see this in the ministry of the Body of Christ as it is described in 1 Corinthians 12. The prophetic anointing is one of the means by which the Lord uses us to minister to one another.

21

PROPHECY REVEALS JESUS CHRIST

The prophetic anointing testifies and bears witness to Jesus Christ as Lord.

> And all Israel from Dan to Beersheba knew that Samuel had been established as a prophet of the LORD. Then the Lord appeared again in Shiloh. For the Lord revealed Himself to Samuel in Shiloh by the word of the LORD. (1 Sam. 3:20-21)

Whatever else may happen when God speaks to you—whether encouragement, comfort, confirmation, or instruction—His ultimate purpose is to reveal Himself.

After His resurrection, Jesus spoke to two disciples on the Emmaus Road. Beginning with Moses and all the Prophets, He expounded to them in all the Scriptures the things concerning Himself (Luke 24:27). In another place, Jesus said,

> You search the Scriptures, for in them you think you have eternal life; and these are they which testify of Me. (John 5:39)

It is important to note that, in referring to the ministry of the Holy Spirit who would be poured out upon the Church after Jesus' ascension, Jesus said,

> But when the Helper comes, whom I shall send to
> you from the Father, the Spirit of truth who
> proceeds from the Father, He will testify of Me.
> (John 15:26)

The Holy Spirit will reveal, magnify, and glorify Jesus. This is the first point made by the Apostle Paul as he began his discussion of the manifestations of the Holy Spirit. He emphasized that anyone speaking by the Spirit of God will confess and acknowledge Jesus Christ as Lord (1 Cor. 12:3).

When the angel appeared to John in Chapter 19:10b of the book of *Revelation*, he told John, "Worship God! For the testimony of Jesus is the spirit of prophecy." In Greek, emphasis is often created by placing first in the sentence the word or phrase that is meant to be emphasized. In this sentence, the Apostle John was placing force on the phrase, "the testimony of Jesus." He was saying that the spirit of prophecy testifies about Jesus Christ. Clearly, this applies to the Bible as the Word of God and the standard by which we judge all else. But it also applies to the ministry of the Holy Spirit in the contemporary life of the Church.

The letters of the apostles reaffirm and establish as foundational the truth that those under the influence of the Holy Spirit will acknowledge and confess that Jesus is Lord. Anyone working in the supernatural who does not acknowledge the Lordship of Jesus is a false prophet and of the Antichrist (1 John 4:1-3; 1 Cor. 12:3).

> For I will come to visions and revelations of the
> Lord. (2 Cor. 12:1b)

Visions and revelations reveal Jesus. Spiritual experiences are not meant to point to themselves. They are to strengthen God's people and inspire faith, perseverance, and endurance. They give confirmation and, in some cases, direction. They enhance our fellowship with God, reveal Christ, cause us to know Him, and strengthen us in our walk with God.

Paul used his visions as a tool in his work. He did not focus on visions but rather acted on the messages brought to him in the visions. He "delivered the mail" rather than making a big deal about the "mail truck."

THE GIFTS AND FRUIT OF THE SPIRIT REVEAL CHRIST

The Holy Spirit comes to reveal and glorify Jesus. The "manifestation" of the Holy Spirit is actually the manifestation of Jesus Himself, walking among us and working through us. For the Church to express the fullness of Christ (Eph. 4:13) to this world, it must abound and grow in both the fruit and gifts of the Holy Spirit. The fruit of the Holy Spirit (Gal. 5:22-23) expresses the nature of Christ, His love and holiness. The gifts or manifestations of the Holy Spirit (1 Cor. 12:7-10) express the power and actions of Christ. This is the true biblical context for the supernatural, an atmosphere where followers of Christ walk in His Word (the Bible) and express His nature and power by the fruit and gifts of the Holy Spirit.

The depth and impact of our ministry is in proportion to our faith in response to the grace that has been given.

> Having then gifts differing according to the grace
> that is given to us, let us use them: if prophecy, let
> us prophesy in proportion to our faith. (Rom. 12:6)

These words should encourage anyone starting out on his or her journey into the gifts and workings of the Holy Spirit. The instruction to "prophesy in proportion to our faith" implies that we must grow in our experience. We grow in faith as we grow in grace. Sometimes, we arise and do amazing things. Other times, we simply step out and take "baby steps." The main thing is to be open to the Holy Spirit's leading and have compassion for those around us. This creates a fertile ground for the Spirit to work among us. Faith often grows as love grows.

When we speak of spiritual gifts, we are speaking of the presence of Jesus Christ working among us. We are not focusing on the spectacular and the dramatic although these do occur from time to time. But mostly, we look for those unobtrusive and often unnoticed acts of the Holy Spirit working in the background and which flow among us as life and grace, quietly yet deeply touching and blessing the lives of those around us. It is those daily, obscure, and non-spectacular acts of obedience that strengthen the Church. They flow out of the individual's desire to be used of God and his or her willingness to reach out to people with love and compassion.

22

KEEPING PROPHECY IN A HEALTHY CONTEXT

The spirits of the prophets are subject to the prophets.

—1 CORINTHIANS 14:32.

YOU CAN BE YOURSELF.

Prophecy is supernatural, but it does not have to feel that way. The "supernatural-ness" is often determined by context and timing as well as by content. The Lord's word is in the content while the style will usually represent the personality of the person giving the word. You can be yourself; you don't have to act strange or take on a different personality.

YOU CAN SPEAK IN A CONVERSATIONAL TONE.

Generally speaking, we can move in the supernatural presence of the Holy Spirit in the normal, conversational tone of everyday life. This is one of the keys to moving in the Holy Spirit on the job, in school, on the street, and in the marketplace. You can be emotional or non-emotional. You can be enthusiastically zealous, or you can be quiet and reserved. The key is to be genuine and real. Sometimes, God's work is seen as obviously and patently supernatural. Other times, it can be hidden and unnoticed because it is defined by the context and timing and may be significant only to those to whom it is directed.

A PERSON MOVING IN PROPHECY SHOULD NOT BE PASSIVE

The spirits of the prophets are subject to the prophets.

—1 CORINTHIANS 14:32

This verse deals with two problems: emotionalism and passivity. Emotions, such as joy and enthusiasm, are good. But emotionalism tends to be emotions posing as or substituting for the Holy Spirit. This generally tends to quench the Holy Spirit. Emotions represent our response to God's presence.

The verse above also deals with the problem of passivity. "The spirit of the prophet is subject to the prophet" means a person should not put his mind and thoughts in neutral, waiting for "something" to take over. Demonic counterfeits, the occult, and false religions work on the principle of passivity. We see it in meditation as practiced by Eastern religions and in the demonic ceremonies of animistic cultures. Allowing your mind's thoughts to go into neutral and your mind to be "blank" opens the door to demonic spirits who take control.

By contrast, the Spirit of God works together with us while our faculties are at work and engaged. The Holy Spirit works through our spirits, and our spirits are subject to us. There are times when the Holy Spirit will move forcibly upon us—as in unusual revivals—but, generally speaking, He will be gentle and lead us rather than drive us. He requires our cooperation and our active involvement rather than a limp vessel with a passive mind.

WE PROPHESY IN PART

For we know in part and we prophesy in part.

—1 CORINTHIANS 13:9

For now we see in a mirror dimly...

—1 CORINTHIANS 13:12A

Paul has reminded us that we are not infallible and that our knowledge is limited. A person moving in prophecy will generally be given only a glimpse of the issues about which he speaks. We may not fully comprehend or understand the implications of the words we give.

PROPHECY SHOULD BE JUDGED

Do not quench the Spirit. Do not despise prophecies. Test all things; hold fast what is good.

—1 THESSALONIANS 5:19-21

Let... prophets speak, and let the others judge.

—1 CORINTHIANS 14:29

Because we are human, we have to deal with the principle of mixture. We make mistakes. Within proven Christian fellowship, our ministry and words should be pure and clearly from God. However, we sometimes let the imaginations of our own heart blend in with the prophetic word and create mixture. This produces the need to test and evaluate whether a word is from God or from man... or a mixture of both.

The devil can also be the motivating source of a word or activity. This is why a prophetic word or any ministry must be evaluated by the written Word of God and discerned by those who are spiritually mature.

Prophecy usually confirms issues that a person has already been dealing with or has been considering. It should not give direction "out of the blue." A person should not accept a word with which he does not identify. He should reject it if he thinks it is wrong or place it in his "pending file" to be evaluated again later. A person should not make a decision based on a prophetic word alone. He should have an inner witness or a confirmation from fellow Christians or spiritual leaders. Prophecy must be harmonious with and not contradict the Bible.

Prophecy, like preaching, does not replace the Bible, nor does it stand on the same level as Scripture. It must be judged or evaluated the same as a sermon or any other word of instruction or exhortation. The Bible is the written Word of God and is the standard by which prophecy and all ministry, church doctrine, and practice should be judged (Gal. 1:6-9; 2 Pet. 1:16-21; Acts 17:11). In testing prophecy or any other word of ministry, we must consider the following:

- Is it harmonious with Scripture?
- Does the recipient of the word identify with it, and does he or she have an inner witness to the truth of the word?
- Are fellow Christians or spiritual leaders able to confirm the word?
- Does the word reflect the love and peace of Christ?

PROPHESYING SHOULD NOT BE USED TO MANIPULATE OR CONTROL.

And they cast their lots, and the lot fell to Matthias.
And he was numbered with the twelve apostles.

—ACTS 1:26

In choosing a man to take Judas' place among the twelve apostles, the group prayed and then "cast their lots." Each man gave his thoughts, and they came to a consensus regarding who was to be chosen. They did what seemed good to them and to the Holy Spirit.

Church leaders should have prophetic insight (Prov. 29:18; Acts 15:28). Leaders need to walk with God, know His heart, and be sensitive to the Holy Spirit's leading. Prophetic words often have a part in making decisions, appointing leaders, and commissioning ministries. But church leaders should not govern by prophecy. Healthy leadership and decision-making require discussion, deliberation, and consensus. It requires checks and balances and looking at all sides of an issue. When a leader tries to govern by prophecy, he subtly intimidates others into submitting to the direction he has chosen. Churches run into problems when members of its ruling council are muzzled and afraid to bring up pertinent issues or express their opinions or challenge what's being presented, especially in controversial matters.

Prophecy should not be used to control and manipulate individuals. A person engaging in this abuse ends up speaking out of the imaginations of his own heart and with misguided, if not evil, motives.

WE SHOULD NOT FORCE PEOPLE TO ACCEPT OUR WORDS.

A person giving a prophetic word must allow the recipient freedom to test the word and to accept or reject the word. We should not coerce a person to act beyond what he or she has grace to do. We should not force a person to receive our words if the person does not identify with or witness to their accuracy. We must allow the person freedom to reject the word and go his or her own way and face the consequences, whether blessing for making the right decision, or discipline for resisting the Lord.

We should prevent excesses and abuses that harm the reputation of the prophetic ministry.

You should not prophesy every time you get a thought or feeling.

You should not prophesy things you ought to communicate from yourself. Don't prophesy what should be given as an exhortation, counsel, personal input, or merely your opinion.

Prophecy should not be used as a substitute for personal confrontation. Some people attribute to God what they themselves would like to say. They put the other person in the psychologically uncomfortable position of having to disagree with God.

It is best not to prophesy in situations where there is conflict. People will not accept it. If it's wrong, it is soulish or carnal and not spiritual. If it's right and a true word, it will end up as "pearls before swine" and will be trampled on (Matt. 7:6).

DON'T TRY TO FULFILL THE PROPHECY YOURSELF; LET GOD DO IT.

> *Then the men of David said to him, "This is the day of which the LORD said to you, 'Behold, I will deliver*

your enemy into your hand, that you may do to him as it seems good to you.' And David arose and secretly cut off a corner of Saul's robe. And he said to his men, "The LORD forbid that I should do this thing to my master, the LORD's anointed, to stretch out my hand against him, seeing he is the anointed of the LORD."

—1 SAMUEL 24:4-6

Abishai [acting on the same promise quoted by David's men in the verse above] said to David, "God has delivered your enemy into your hand this day. Now therefore, please, let me strike him at once with the spear, right to the earth..."

—1 SAMUEL 26:8A

This principle applies to those who *receive* a prophetic word. We must allow God to fulfill His own words rather than trying to do it ourselves. Waiting on God's timing requires faith, patience, and godly character.

Abraham is the first example that comes to my mind. He was promised a son, but instead of waiting on God to fulfill this word, Abraham tried to do it on his own. He produced Ishmael by his own flesh rather than waiting on Isaac, the son of promise (Gen. 16).

The prophetic word to David was that God would deliver his enemies into his hands. In the two verses quoted above, King Saul was on a campaign to find and kill David. In the first example, David was hiding in the recesses of a cave where Saul just happened to enter to "use the restroom." In the second example, Saul was asleep in his camp. In both cases, David could have killed Saul while he was in defenseless and vulnerable positions. In both cases, David's men encouraged him, based on a prophetic word to kill Saul. They whispered, "This is your chance to fulfill the prophecy. Saul is your enemy, and you can kill him now!" David, however, knew in his heart that this was not the time or the manner. He would not enlist his own flesh or the devil's methods to accomplish God's purpose. He would wait for God's hand, God's timing, and God's way.

A word from God not only encourages and strengthens us, but also, at times, it tests us (Psa. 105:19). A word from God does not necessarily make life easier. Sometimes, it involves waiting, and it requires faith and patience—that is, steadfast perseverance. In the words of an Old Testament prophet, "Though it tarries, wait for it" (Hab. 2:3).

KEEPING BALANCE

Each aspect of church life has to be in focus without becoming *the* focus. The tendency of human nature, however, is to take an individual aspect one has experienced and to sensationalize it, go to an extreme with it, overemphasize it, and treat it as a cure-all.

When Christians experience a new and amazing gift, they tend to think they have reached the pinnacle of their experience in the Holy Spirit, not realizing there is so much more to experience and so many more "rooms" in the household of God. Christians in the traditional mainline denominations thought they had "arrived" when they were introduced to and received the baptism in the Holy Spirit. Healing evangelists came through, and many assumed this was the height of New Testament Christianity. Then, Christians began to experience the other manifestations of the Holy Spirit and the Ephesians 4 ministries of apostles, prophets, and real New Testament evangelists. Our desire is to see the Church mature and grow in all aspects.

Part 3

PRAYING IN THE SPIRIT

23

PRAYING IN TONGUES: A MANIFESTATION OF THE HOLY SPIRIT

But the manifestation of the Spirit is given to each one for the profit of all... to another the working of miracles, to another prophecy, to another discerning of spirits, to another different kinds of tongues...

—1 CORINTHIANS 12:7, 10B

In 1 Corinthians 12 and 14, Paul made it very clear that praying in tongues is one of the manifestations of the Holy Spirit and not some strange and useless phenomenon that the Corinthians contrived and sneaked into the church when God wasn't looking. God placed this gift in the Church as a practical and useful tool in the believer's prayer life. Therefore, we must ask the question, "What does this mean for me?"

In contemporary Christianity, praying in tongues is often misrepresented, abused, ignored, and misunderstood. The traditional Pentecostal churches have tended to practice it only during an emotional high during worship services, while failing to recognize it as a regular part of their daily and normal prayer life. Traditional denominational and evangelical churches have avoided the subject altogether or have spoken harshly against the gift as a reaction to what they consider strange behavior of those who practice it.

It is important, therefore, that we form our understanding based on principles expressed in the Bible rather than forming our beliefs as a reaction to abuses. To form a doctrine on any subject, one must look at everything the Bible has to say on that subject and formulate a position that encompasses all the related Scripture verses, without excluding any. We err when we accept verses that support our position while ignoring or rejecting the verses we don't like. This study will take into consideration all of the related verses, both positive and negative. Our goal is to understand what the New Testament Christians experienced and to make that experience our own.

The objective is not to argue with or prove anything to those who disagree but rather to encourage those who are already favorably disposed and to give to them a clearer understanding of the very practical, useful, and spiritual purposes God intended when He set this manifestation of the Holy Spirit into the Church. This study will help us to understand its role in helping the believer to grow in spirit and enter the presence of God in a deeper experience of intercessory prayer and praise. We will see that praying in the Spirit is a positive and wonderful tool placed in the Church by God Himself. We will discuss the nature and purpose of tongues and will attempt to answer many of the typical questions that are usually asked.

THE PRESENCE OF TONGUES IN THE NEW TESTAMENT CHURCH

"Tongues" is the King James word for "languages." It is the supernatural ability to pray in another language—either earthly or heavenly—by means of the Holy Spirit. It is a working tool, an instrument of prayer, intercession, praise, and worship. The Bible references below show us how pervasive was the presence of tongues in the early Christian Church. Tongues were present in the following settings:

Pentecost

> *And they were all filled with the Holy Spirit and began to speak with other tongues as the Holy Spirit gave them utterance.*
>
> —ACTS 2:1-4

Samaria

(See Acts 8:14-19)

When the Samaritans received the Holy Spirit, Simon saw something beyond the joy, miracles, healings, and deliverance from demons that accompanied the salvation experiences in verses 5-8. He witnessed something that was new, real, and evident; otherwise, he would not have offered money to buy the power to impart it. My personal opinion is that these people— following the pattern of Acts 2:1-4, 10:44-48, and 19:1-7—prayed in tongues, prophesied, and began themselves to move in the supernatural power and gifts of the Holy Spirit.

Cornelius' household

> *While Peter was still speaking these words, the Holy Spirit fell upon all those who heard the word... for they heard them speak with tongues and magnify God.*
>
> —ACTS 10:44-48

The Church at Ephesus

> *And when Paul had laid hands on them, the Holy Spirit came upon them, and they spoke with tongues and prophesied.*
>
> —ACTS 19:1-7

The Apostle Paul

> *I thank my God I speak with tongues more than you all.*
>
> —1 CORINTHIANS 14:18

It is interesting to note that the book of *Acts* makes no reference at all to Paul's praying in tongues, yet from his writings, it is evident that praying in tongues was a vital part of his Christian walk.

The Church at Corinth

> *...whenever you come together, each of you... has a tongue...*
>
> —1 CORINTHIANS 14:26

The book of *Acts* makes no mention of the Corinthians praying in tongues, yet it is obvious from the book of *1 Corinthians* that they did pray in tongues and move in the gifts of the Spirit.

PRAYING IN TONGUES IS A MANIFESTATION OF THE HOLY SPIRIT

The Holy Spirit was at work among all the churches of the New Testament. Tongues is listed among the manifestations of the

Spirit and, as such, was present wherever the Spirit of God was at work in the early Church. The same should be true for us today (see 1 Cor. 14:26; Heb. 2:1-4; Gal. 3:1-5).

Praying in tongues is a manifestation of the Holy Spirit that was set in the Church by God Himself and was a common practice among early Christians. I will discuss in more detail the nature and purpose of this practical and positive tool the Lord has given to aid us in our spiritual walk.

24

TONGUES: A DEEPER LEVEL OF SERVING GOD IN PRAYER

Praying in tongues enables us to participate at a deeper level in intercession for the purposes of God around the world.

...praying always with all prayer and supplication in the Spirit, being watchful to this end with all perseverance and supplication for all the saints... (Eph. 6:18)

Likewise the Spirit also helps in our weaknesses. For we do not know what we should pray for as we ought, but the Spirit Himself makes intercession for us with groanings which cannot be uttered. Now He who searches the hearts knows what the mind of the Spirit is, because He makes intercession for the saints according to the will of God. (Rom. 8:26-27)

For he who prays in a tongue does not speak to men but to God, for no one understands him; however, in the spirit he speaks mysteries. (1 Cor. 14:2)

...how he was caught up into Paradise and heard inexpressible words, which it is not lawful for a man to utter. (2 Cor. 12:4)

Now when He had taken the scroll, the four living creatures and the twenty-four elders fell down before the Lamb, each having a harp, and golden bowls full of incense, which are the prayers of the saints. (Rev. 5:8)

Christians often fail to realize the real importance and necessity of prayer. Many remain at a shallow level in their prayer experience, not realizing the depths that can be attained as they enter the presence of God. One of the mysteries of prayer is that people think they know what it is while, in fact, real prayer is probably one of the least-understood spiritual experiences. So many Christians have walked into the foyer and think they have experienced the whole house. Not only do they fail to enter the house itself, but they also fail to realize there are things to do in the house.

What God does on earth, He accomplishes through the prayers of the saints. This is evident from all biblical exhortations to prayer. God has chosen us to be involved in His plan and has called us to work together with Him in His program for the earth. In the same way that the responsibility for the proclamation of the gospel lies with the Church—rather than with angels—so also is the responsibility and privilege God has given the Church to help Him accomplish His purposes on earth through prayer. We cannot say, "God will do what He wants to without me." We cannot say, "Whatever will be will be." This attitude fails to recognize our part in the process. It fails to recognize that God moves upon us through prayer, intercession, praise, and proclamation to help fulfill His plan. Whatever God does on earth is preceded by prayer somewhere. He shows us what He plans to do, and we pray it into its fulfillment.

In Daniel 9:1-3 and 9:16-19, God revealed to Daniel through the writings of Jeremiah that Israel would be delivered after 70 years of captivity. Daniel was among the captives when he received this revelation of God's will. He did not sit back and say, "Well, God is going to deliver us in a few years, so I can just relax and wait." On the contrary, once he saw God's plan and knew God's will, he began to fast, pray, and seek God for its fulfillment. He worked together with God to help bring it about. Daniel 10 gives us a glimpse of the warfare in the heavenlies and shows us how our prayers help "give ammunition" to the heavenly hosts who fight with spirit rulers or principalities and powers (Eph. 6:10-19).

Once we understand the principles just stated above, we can begin to realize the importance of praying in the Spirit. God wants to use us to pray and intercede for many things that He is doing around the world. He cannot inform us intellectually of everything He is doing, and He cannot let us know every detail of those wonders and mysteries He is accomplishing around the world. He does not even inform us of most of the details around our own lives. We would not be able to handle it. Therefore, tongues—that is, the supernatural ability to pray in an unknown language by the Holy Spirit—is God's way of delivering Himself from man's limitedness and finiteness of language and intellect. Tongues allows the Holy Spirit to bypass our natural minds and to pray directly through our spirits concerning those issues, events, and purposes that are beyond the realm of our comprehension or which are beyond the bounds of our need to know.

If I pray in a tongue, my spirit prays...

—1 CORINTHIANS 14:14

WHEN YOU PRAY IN TONGUES, YOUR SPIRIT PRAYS

For if I pray in a tongue, my spirit prays, but my understanding is unfruitful. What is the conclusion then? I will pray with the spirit, and I will also pray with the understanding. I will sing with the spirit, and I will also sing with the understanding.

—1 CORINTHIANS 14:14-15

The term, "spiritual gifts," in 1 Corinthians 12:1 is the Greek word, "pneumatikos." It can be translated "spirituals," meaning "that which is spirit by nature and which operates in the realm of spirit." Speaking in tongues is included in this list. Jude 20 speaks of praying "in the Holy Spirit," and 1 Corinthians 14:14 speaks of praying "with the spirit," meaning our own human spirit. Praying in tongues, therefore, is the Holy Spirit working through the human spirit rather than through the mind.

Praying in tongues is just one aspect of praying in the Holy Spirit. All genuine prayer is in the Holy Spirit, but Paul's reference in 1 Corinthians 14:14 speaks specifically of praying in tongues as opposed to his own language. He said, "My spirit prays, but my understanding is unfruitful."

SUBSTITUTING INTELLECT FOR SPIRIT

The prayer life of so many Christians is shallow because they pray only from their head and not from their heart. They have not experienced that release of the spirit that allows them to pour out their soul before the Lord (John 7:37-38). They stay in the realm of the mind and intellect in their Christian walk, and this is reflected in the superficial nature of their prayers.

This type of person tends to be afraid of tongues because they see it as an emotional extreme. My own observation, however, is that the shallow complacency of intellect devoid of the Holy Spirit is a greater problem in Western Christianity than is emotionalism. For every Christian who has fallen into emotional extremes, there are significantly more who sit with minimal spiritual life, going through religious rote and empty ritual.

Churches and Christians who lack real spiritual depth tend to err in one of two directions. One group tends to keep everything at an intellectual level, substituting intellect for spirit, while another group tends to be very emotional, equating emotion with spirituality. Both can quench the Holy Spirit. A third but non-Christian alternative is the "spirit of the world" (1 Cor. 2:12; Eph. 2:2), which is demonic and characterizes the New Age and occult movements.

Intellectualism is offended by tongues because tongues is a work of the Holy Spirit through the human spirit, causing the mind and intellect to take a backseat. Emotionalism can accept tongues but hijacks it and turns it into a soulish experience that actually quenches the human spirit and Holy Spirit. Praying in tongues is neither emotional gibberish nor emotionalism.

If I pray in a tongue, my spirit prays. (1 Cor. 14:14)

And the spirits of the prophets are subject to the prophets. (1 Cor. 14:32)

Let all things be done decently and in order.
(1 Cor. 14:40)

Tongues is not "ecstatic speech" as some have mistakenly translated it. One can pray in tongues calmly, quietly, and in the same manner as one prays in his or her own language. He can pray quietly under his breath in a whisper, in a normal conversational tone, or in a shout with great volume and intensity. When you pray in tongues your spirit prays, and your spirit is subject to you.

Emotionalism occurs when people unwisely wait for some outside force to "take over." People should be in control of themselves when they pray in tongues or move in any of the manifestations of the Holy Spirit (1 Cor. 12:7-11). Paul told the Corinthians that prophets were not to interrupt each other. The spirit of the prophet is subject to the prophet (1 Cor. 14:30-33). Therefore, when he gets a word, he can wait and give it at the appropriate time. The Holy Spirit may, at times, move very strongly upon a person but will not "take over" and force anyone to stand up and speak uncontrollably. The same principle applies to praying in tongues.

The Bible and history show us that there have been and will be times of special revival and visitation when God does unusual and extraordinary things, accompanied by emotion, great joy, and unusual physical manifestations. But still, while emotional reactions may accompany the workings of the Spirit, emotions should not be confused with the Spirit nor seen as a requirement. Emotionalism—that is, when emotions become the goal and focus—actually tend over time to quench the working of the Holy Spirit.

Emotion is a God-given aspect of human nature. It can be a response to God's presence and an instrument through which we express worship and praise. But we should not confuse emotions with the Holy Spirit. After times of unusual manifestations of the Spirit during extraordinary revivals, there is a danger of ritualizing the unusual experiences and perpetuating them artificially. Substituting emotions for the Spirit rings shallow and hollow.

Tongues is meant to be a spiritual experience. It is not primarily intellectual or emotional. Praying in tongues—that is, the supernatural ability to pray in an unknown language by the Holy Spirit—is God's way of delivering Himself from man's limitedness and finiteness of language and intellect. Tongues allows the Holy Spirit to bypass our natural minds and to pray directly through our spirits concerning issues, events, and purposes that are beyond the realm of our comprehension or that are beyond the bounds of our need to know.

If I pray in a tongue, my spirit prays...

—1 CORINTHIANS 14:14

25

STRENGTHENED IN SPIRIT TO REACH OUT TO OTHERS

Pursue love, and desire spiritual gifts...

—1 CORINTHIANS 14:1A

Praying in tongues should not be approached from a solely doctrinal or analytical point of view. It is a magnificent gift and wonderful tool to strengthen our own spiritual lives and to open the door for more effective ministry to others. If we truly love, we will obey the Apostle Paul's command to "desire spiritual gifts."

I pray in tongues because it strengthens my prayer life, strengthens my spirit, and helps release my ability to move in the other gifts of the Spirit. In turn, these gifts will help me to touch others with the compassion, presence, and power of God.

PRAYING IN TONGUES BUILDS UP THE BELIEVER

In 1 Corinthians 2:7-11, Paul listed the manifestations of the Holy Spirit (i.e. spiritual gifts). Each of these gifts works through believers to touch or bless others... except for tongues, which is the only one specifically designed for you to use to build up and strengthen yourself.

> He who speaks in a tongue edifies himself…
> (1 Cor. 14:4a)

> But you, beloved, building yourselves up on your most holy faith, praying in the Holy Spirit.
> (Jude 20)

When you pray in tongues, you edify yourself. The verse, 1 Corinthians 14:4, has been interpreted erroneously to say that praying in tongues was for the immature, ignorant, and unstable. But all Christians need to be edified and built up. Why would you throw away an obvious tool that was placed in your hand for that very purpose? It is not noble or logical to say, "I will seek to build up others, but I will not build up myself." It is proper and necessary that we seek to strengthen ourselves in the Lord.

Paul himself said that he prayed in tongues more than all of the Corinthians (1 Cor. 14:18), and he was a spiritual giant. To say that tongues was for the unstable and immature is actually a powerful argument in favor of tongues. The most serious cases require the most potent medicine, and what works for a person who is weak should do wonders for a person who is healthy.

Praying in tongues is an important step in strengthening your own spirit and releasing you to move more freely in the Holy Spirit. It is a door that opens unto the other manifestations of the Spirit. Tongues is much like a key. A key is not the most important tool around the house, but it is vital in unlocking access to other more important things in the house.

26

PRAYING IN TONGUES AS AN INSTRUMENT OF PRAISE

It came to pass, when the trumpeters and singers were as one, to make one sound to be heard in praising and thanking the Lord, and when they lifted up their voice with the trumpets and cymbals and instruments of music, and praised the Lord... that the house of the Lord, was filled with a cloud, so that the priests could not continue ministering because of the cloud; for the glory of the Lord filled the house of God.

—2 CHRONICLES 5:13-14; SEE ALSO LUKE 9:34-35

My wife, Laurel, and I once witnessed an unusual manifestation of God's presence during praise and worship at a conference in California in the early 1970s. There were about 300 people standing with hands lifted to the Lord and singing praises in tongues. It was a beautiful, harmonious blend of voices rising to the Lord like a symphony orchestra. As I looked about, I saw what appeared to be a misty cloud that filled the room. My initial reaction was to rub my eyes, thinking there was a problem with my vision. But then, I saw the leaders excitedly moving about on stage and pointing out over

the congregation. Everyone at that moment realized we were witnessing the cloud of God's glory being manifested in response to the praise. This was an awesome experience. Ralph Mahoney, the director of World Missionary
Assistance Plan (World MAP), wrote about this event in a subsequent publication of the organization's magazine.

Our experience that night reminded us that praying and singing in tongues can be significant instruments of praise.

AN APPRECIATION OF PRAISE

To appreciate tongues as an instrument of praise, you must first have an appreciation of praise itself. Otherwise, the discussion will remain in the realm of dry technicalities. Therefore, I would like to discuss praise briefly before discussing tongues as it relates to praise.

Praise can be quiet reverence, speaking silently from the heart, but it should also include outward expressions of exuberant and joyous enthusiasm. It is not simply a feeling or ritual but an act of worship in which the human spirit expresses itself through voice and body to give thanksgiving, honor, and glory to God. Praise should not be limited to inner, silent thought but should be an expression of the whole person, verbally and physically reaching out to God. We should have the same enthusiasm for God that fans show for their sports teams. Why should we "make the rafters ring" for a ball team but remain lifeless and frozen when we approach God?

We see many various expressions of praise in the Bible. We see the children of God lifting their hands and voices in praise. We see them dancing before the Lord, clapping their hands, and leaping for joy. We see them singing songs to God, sometimes a cappella and sometimes with every form of musical instrument. We hear them reciting to the Lord all His wonderful deeds and mighty acts. We see the people spreading palm branches before Jesus as He made His triumphal entry into Jerusalem.

Worship is not a cold solemnity we call reverence but a living and joyous expression of honor and love to the living and very present God before whom we stand and to whom we lift our voices. It should not be a passive audience listening to a worship team on stage nor just a collection of people worshipping as isolated individuals but a body of believers joined as one, as a family, to make one sound that rises to God as a beautiful symphony.

Praise is more than warm Sunday morning songs we sing prior to the sermon. It is the people of God dynamically entering the presence of God, touching Him with their spirits, pouring forth love and honor to Him, and in turn, experiencing the presence of God that inhabits those praises. Like prayer, it is also a means by which God allows His people to be dynamically involved in the release of His awesome work upon the earth. This is evident in many of the psalms and in the praise paragraphs that are interspersed throughout the book of *Revelation*. Praise is an acknowledgment of the King and His coming Kingdom. No wonder Jesus said, "If these were to keep silent, the very stones would cry out!"

> *And I heard, as it were, the voice of a great multitude, as the sound of many waters and as the sound of mighty thunderings, saying, "Alleluia! For the Lord God Omnipotent reigns!"*

> —REVELATION 19:6

27

THE SIGNIFICANCE OF TONGUES IN RELATION TO PRAISE

...and they were all filled with the Holy Spirit and begin to speak with other tongues [languages] as the Spirit gave them utterance. Then they [Jews from foreign nations] were all amazed and marveled, saying to one another, "Look, are not all these who speak Galileans? And how is it that we hear, each in our own language?...we hear them speaking in our own tongues the wonderful works of God.

— ACTS 2:4, 8, 11B

People who do not understand the purpose of tongues use in 1 Corinthians 14:14-23 as a basis for forbidding them altogether. The praise in tongues on the Day of Pentecost was not meant to edify the listeners but was a sign that captured their attention and drew them to the gathering. The foreigners thought these worshipers were drunk. This is a good illustration of what Paul meant in 1 Corinthians 14:23 where he said that an uninformed person or unbeliever may think you're crazy if you're speaking in tongues. The Day of Pentecost exemplified Paul's teaching that prayer and praise in tongues are directed to

God and not to man. Tongues edify the speaker but may, in some cases, be a sign to the listeners (1 Cor. 14:22a).

The crowd heard their own languages and knew these people were praising God. However, the praises did not explain anything to the listeners but rather got their attention and raised the question, "What does this mean?" Peter then stood up and gave the sermon that provided the answer. The "10,000 words in tongues" did not edify the crowd but did give praise to God and served as a sign to gather the multitude to hear Peter's message.

A FORM OF PRAISE WE SEE IN *PSALMS*

The worshipers on the Day of Pentecost were speaking to God, recounting and rehearsing His mighty acts and thanking Him for all He had done. This is a form of praise we find throughout *Psalms*. Praying in tongues enables us, like the Psalmist, to "speak the wonderful works of God" but supernaturally in earthly languages (tongues of men) or in heavenly languages (tongues of angels).

> Though I speak with the tongues of men or of angels... (1 Cor. 13:1a)

> Who can speak of [utter] the mighty deeds of the LORD? Who can show forth all His praise?
> (Psa. 106:2)

> Oh that men would praise the LORD for His goodness, and for His wonderful works to the children of men! (Psa. 107:8, 15, 21, 31)

Oh give thanks to the Lord... Make known His deeds among the peoples. Sing to Him, sing praises to Him. Speak of all His wonders [wondrous works]! (Psa. 105:1-2)

"SPIRITUAL SONGS" ARE SONGS OF THE SPIRIT

What is it then... I will sing with the spirit, and I will also sing with the understanding... for indeed you give thanks well...

— 1 CORINTHIANS 14:15, 17

...be filled with the Spirit, speaking to one another in psalms and hymns and spiritual songs, singing and making melody in your heart to the Lord.

— EPHESIANS 5:18B-19

...in psalms and hymns and spiritual songs, singing with grace in your hearts to the Lord.

— COLOSSIANS 3:16B

The verses above speak of psalms, hymns, and spiritual songs. "Psalms" refers to songs that take their general character from the book of *Psalms*, usually accompanied by musical instruments and repeating the wonderful works of God. "Hymns" speaks of songs of praise. In early Greek writings from Homer on down, it referred to praise of heroes and conquerors. "Spiritual songs" are songs sung in the Spirit, a person's spirit singing by the Holy Spirit.

"Spiritual songs" is a translation of the Greek words, *hodais pneumatikos*. *Hodais* is the generic term for "songs," whether praise songs or songs about any other subject. *Pneumatikos* is the word for "spiritual" or "belonging to spirit" and is the same word used in 1 Corinthians 12:1 referring to "spiritual gifts," meaning "that which operates in the realm of spirit." Paul was not using the term, "spiritual songs," in the same way our contemporary culture uses it to refer to "spirituals" (i.e. gospel songs) as opposed to "secular" music. In this context (1 Cor. 14), he was talking about spiritual gifts and, in particular, tongues. "Spiritual" here refers to spirit as opposed to the mind and singing in tongues as opposed to singing with the understanding. "Spiritual songs," therefore, refers to the Holy Spirit working through the human spirit, singing in tongues.

> I will sing in the spirit, and I will also sing with the understanding. (1 Cor. 14:15b)

GOD IS GREAT AND GREATLY TO BE PRAISED

Praying in the Spirit enables us to enter a deeper dimension of praise and worship. To appreciate tongues, we need to appreciate praise itself. Previously, I referred to the many various expressions of praise we see in Scripture, such as lifting hands and voices in praise, dancing before the Lord, clapping hands, leaping for joy, and singing songs to God, both a cappella and with every form of musical instrument. We now add tongues to that list. The psalmist said, "Great is the LORD and greatly to be praised!" (Psa. 48:1). We, therefore, should praise Him greatly and with every tool He has made available to us.

> *Oh for a thousand tongues to sing*
> *my great Redeemer's praise,*
> *the glories of my God and King,*
> *the triumphs of His grace.*
>
> —CHARLES WESLEY

28

QUESTIONS THAT TYPICALLY ARISE AROUND THE DISCUSSION OF TONGUES

DO I HAVE TO PRAY IN TONGUES?

A friend of mine once said, "You don't have to; you get to." Most Pentecostals and Charismatics believe that praying in tongues is the evidence of being baptized in the Holy Spirit. I will not be dogmatic on this point, but I do believe we should follow the example set in the book of *Acts*. They prayed in tongues, prophesied, and moved in the supernatural power of God. Why should we resist or see as negative anything that is from the Holy Spirit. It might be possible for a person to be filled with the Spirit without praying in tongues, but I believe that every person who is filled with the Holy Spirit can and should pray in tongues. Praying in the Spirit opens up so many avenues in one's spiritual life and serves so many useful purposes. It does not make you better than anyone else, but it is a wonderful tool to help you reach higher into your own spiritual potential.

PRAYING IN TONGUES IS THE DOOR TO THE OTHER MANIFESTATIONS OF THE SPIRIT.

The baptism in the Holy Spirit—that is, being filled with the Holy Spirit—releases your spirit to move more freely in the Holy Spirit. Praying in the Spirit is a means of exercising your spirit and helping you to be more sensitive to the Holy Spirit, thus releasing your ability to work with Him in other manifestations and gifts of the Spirit. Generally speaking, people who reject tongues also fail to experience a real release in the other supernatural gifts of the Spirit.

IN THE NEW TESTAMENT, PRAYING IN TONGUES WAS NOT SOME UNUSUAL AND RARE PHENOMENON THAT OCCURRED ONLY ONCE FOR EACH PERSON AT THE INITIAL INFILLING OF THE HOLY SPIRIT BUT WAS A COMMON, DAILY PRACTICE OF THE PRAYING BELIEVER.

In 1 Corinthians 14:18, Paul said, "I speak." He did not say, "I spoke." He used the present tense, which in Greek, refers to progressive or continuing action. This verse, along with the following verse, implies that Paul prayed a great deal in tongues outside the church in his daily prayer life. Praying in tongues was a vital aspect of Paul's exhortation that we should be "praying always with all prayer and supplication in the Spirit" (Eph. 6:18a). A person can pray in his own language or in tongues anywhere, anytime, and no matter what else he or she is doing.

TO FORBID TONGUES IS TO DISOBEY A DIRECT BIBLICAL COMMAND.

Therefore, brethren, desire earnestly to prophesy, and do not forbid to speak with tongues.

—1 CORINTHIANS 14:39

THERE ARE TWO MAJOR CATEGORIES OF TONGUES.

This perspective is drawn from an objective look at all the verses on the subject and clarifies certain verses. One category is the simple manifestation of the Spirit used for prayer, intercession, praise and worship, or edification to strengthen the believer. This does not require an interpreter, and there is no limit to the number of people who can be praying together in this fashion (1 Cor. 14: 2-4).

The second category is the ministry of tongues. This refers to an individual being moved upon by the Spirit to speak a message in tongues to or before the congregation while all others listen silently. This is to be followed by an interpretation and is limited to "two or three at the most" (1 Cor. 14:27-28). If there is no one who will interpret, the person is to "keep silent"—that is, not give the message in tongues to the church but to "speak to himself and to God" in his own language or in tongues.

"TWO OR THREE AT THE MOST" (1 COR. 14:27)

This limitation is placed on the messages in tongues addressed to the church. There is no limit placed on the number who can pray in tongues in regular prayer, praise, worship, and intercession. Congregational singing and worship in tongues can be very beautiful. It is interesting to note that, in every example in the book of *Acts*, there are more than three people praying in tongues. There were at least 120 people praying in tongues simultaneously on the Day of Pentecost (Acts 2:1-4; 1:15). In Cornelius' household, there was a house full of people praying in the Spirit at the same time (Acts 10:44-46). There were 12 at Ephesus (Acts 19:6-7).

KEEP SILENT? (1 COR. 14:28)

"Silent" here—as well as in 1 Corinthians 14:34 regarding women—is not to be taken in the absolute sense. The term, "silent," is implying here that a person should not address his message to the church without an interpreter. If there is no interpreter, he should be quiet in the sense of not giving the word to the church. But "let him speak to himself and to God" in his own languages or in tongues.

The meaning is used in a similar manner in 1 Corinthians 14:34 regarding women keeping silent in church. It is obvious from 1 Corinthians 11:5 that Paul expected women to speak up in prayer, prophecy, exhortation, and all of the other gifts of the Spirit. Paul was not saying that women or tongues should be silent in the absolute sense.

IS TONGUES THE LEAST GIFT? (1 COR. 12:28)

People mistakenly infer this from 1 Corinthians 12:28 where it is last in a list. The list here denotes ministries (1 Cor. 12:18, 28). Tongues may be a lesser ministry, but it is not a lesser personal gift. Each of these gift-ministries is a "member" set in the Body of Christ by God Himself, regardless of order of importance. God does nothing that is not important, and He does nothing that is unnecessary. Praying in tongues was designed by the wisdom of God to serve very practical and useful purposes. Verse 18 says that all of the various gifts are like members (i.e. limbs) of a body. They were all set in the Body of Christ by God Himself, and they all please Him.

We must, therefore, beware of arrogance that despises

tongues or any other work of the Holy Spirit. We should never despise what God was pleased to institute.

Tongues is not the least gift. It is probably one of the most important personal gifts. As I stated earlier, Tongues is much like a key. A key is not the most important tool around the house, but it is vital in unlocking access to other more important things in the house. Even if tongues were the least gift, that would be no reason to avoid it or think of it as bad, something to fear, or something to "throw out the window," saying, "I have no need of thee" (1 Cor. 12:21-24).

IS PAUL SAYING TO PROPHESY INSTEAD OF PRAYING IN TONGUES? (1 COR. 14:5)

The Greek phrase, "mallon de," in the King James Version is mistakenly translated as "but rather." While this translation can be technically correct, in this context it represents a grammatical irregularity—that is, a command followed by a contradiction. It should be translated as "but more," which is also technically correct and more logical for the context. The newer translations as a whole translate it as "but more."

> I want you to pray in tongues, but moreover
> [mallon de] that you go on and prophesy.
> (1 Cor. 14:5)

> Be zealous for spiritual gifts, and especially
> [mallon de] prophecy. (1 Cor. 14:1)

In both verses, the "mallon de" wants to add something. In neither verse does it negate the directive that precedes it.

DO ALL SPEAK WITH TONGUES? (1 COR. 12:30)

All do not have the ministry of tongues in which messages are given to the Body to be interpreted, but all can pray in tongues for personal devotionals, prayer, intercession, praise, and worship. The same principle applies to both prophecy and tongues.

Paul asked in 1 Corinthians 12:29, "Are all prophets?" The obvious and expected answer is "no." All do not function in the *office* of prophet, nor do all function in the specialized ministry of prophecy (Rom. 12:6). However, Paul does say that "you can all prophesy" (1 Cor. 14:24, 31) and that we should desire and seek to prophesy (1 Cor. 14:1). So, all are not prophets, meaning not all hold that office or move in prophecy as a ministry, yet all can prophesy.

In the same way, all do not have the ministry of tongues in which messages in tongues are addressed to the church (1 Cor. 12:30), yet all can pray in tongues (1 Cor. 14:5).

HAS PRAYING IN TONGUES CEASED?

> ...*but whether there are prophecies, they will fail; whether there are tongues, they will cease; whether there is knowledge, it will vanish away. For now we know in part, and we prophesy in part. But when that which is perfect has come, then that which is in part will be done away... For now we see in a mirror, dimly, but then face to face.*
>
> —1 CORINTHIANS 13:8-10, 12

Tongues will cease when that which is perfect has come. "That which is perfect" refers to the age to come. Paul was comparing the "now" and the "then." We are still in the "now" era. The "then" refers to a time when everything will be perfected and when that which is in part shall be done away with. We shall see face to face and shall know fully even as we are fully known. That time has not yet arrived. Tongues will not cease until Jesus returns.

Meanwhile, all of the gifts and ministries of the Holy Spirit that were operating in the early Church should be working in the Church today. According to Ephesians 4:11-13, the apostles and prophets shall continue until the Church attains "the knowledge of the Son of God, to a perfect man, to the measure of the stature of the fullness of Christ." Thus, tongues, prophets, apostles, and all of the other operations and manifestations of the Holy Spirit that were experienced by the early Christians are available to us today and will continue until the Church is perfected—that is, until Jesus returns.

29

Don't Tongues Cause Division?

T he people in our Baptist church loved the Lord, but I was not satisfied with the routine. I had a hunger to know and walk with Jesus in the same way as those early Christians I read about in the Bible. The Lord heard the cry of my heart, and I received the baptism in the Holy Spirit in the early days of the Charismatic Movement in 1967 when I was 17 years old.

The Lord was pouring out His Spirit upon people in all church denominations in the United States and around the world. Christians were receiving the baptism in the Holy Spirit and were experiencing a renewal in the gifts of the Holy Spirit, including healing and praying in tongues. I personally witnessed miracles of healing in those days and experienced the excitement and enthusiasm one would expect with the discovery of such new-found treasures. Multitudes rejoiced to know that Jesus Christ was working in the Church and on the earth in the same intimate way He did in the Bible. People were justifiably excited, and there were many whose zeal may have exceeded their wisdom.

Truth can cause division

Not everyone was happy with these developments, and it was not uncommon to hear people say, "Don't get involved with tongues. They cause division." Relational stresses did occur, but the reasons are more complex than simply "tongues."

Orthodox Christianity will naturally respond to perceived heresies when they arise. Therefore, divisions may occur when good people react justifiably to an evil doctrine or practice that tries to invade the Church. But we must also realize that truth itself can cause division when people react to it in a hostile manner. Therefore, division does not necessarily indicate that the message causing the division is wrong or evil. While the New Testament condemns division arising from heresy and self-will, it also gives examples of division and strife arising because people rejected God's Word and stumbled over truth.

Truth can bring division and even confusion when men reject it. The ministry of the Apostle Paul is an example of how conflict and strife can be the results of a negative reaction to positive truth. The following verses show how this happened to Paul as he preached the gospel message across the Roman Empire.

> These men [Paul and his company] do exceedingly trouble our city [are throwing our city into confusion], and they teach customs which are not lawful for us… to receive or observe.
> (Acts 16:20b-21)

> …there arose a great commotion about the Way.
> (Acts 19:23)

> So the whole city was filled with confusion… Some therefore cried one thing and some another, for the assembly was confused, and most of them did not know why they had come together.
> (Acts 19:29a, 32)

> For we have found this man [the Apostle Paul] a plague [a real pest] and a fellow who stirs up dissension among all the Jews throughout the world... (Acts 24:5)

We must emphasize that the Apostle Paul never deliberately tried to incite trouble. The gospel is a message of peace, and it will produce peace in the individual and society that believe and act upon it. But the Word of God is rarely received in a neutral manner. Truth carries with it the ability to bring joy, peace, and blessing. But it sometimes confronts people with realities they are not yet willing to face and so has the potential to create tension. The messenger will often find himself either loved or hated.

Therefore, we must walk in compassion, wisdom, and love and do everything in our power to bless and not hurt God's people. If they are going to be offended, let them be offended by the truth itself and not by our lack of wisdom or our foolishness in how we present it. We should not be arrogant, insensitive, unwise, or unloving but walk humbly and with grace. But even when we have conducted ourselves in the wisest possible way with exemplary love and patience, there will still be those who are offended by truth. There will be those for whom certain truths will be unpalatable, no matter how much "sweetener" we add and no matter how much we disguise it in the comfortable fit of the person's culture. We must do all we can to walk in love and wisdom but also be prepared for those who reject the truth and sometimes us along with it.

Praying in tongues is one aspect of our spiritual experience that has been a controversial topic. We are thankful for this valuable prayer tool, and we encourage others to practice it. But we do not force it on anyone, nor do we condemn or judge anyone who disagrees. Praying in tongues does not make me better than anyone else, but it does make my own prayer life better than it would be otherwise.

THE APOSTOLIC TRADITIONS

> *...keep the traditions just as I delivered them to you.*
>
> —1 CORINTHIANS 11:2B

Tongues is part of the traditions passed down by Paul and the other apostles. We should hold firmly to these traditions and not lay them aside in favor of the ones developed subsequently by those destitute of the gifts. We must avoid division caused by doctrine and traditions that are contrary to what Paul and the early apostles taught (Rom. 16:17), but we must embrace the doctrines and traditions that were practiced by the early Christians and be willing to pay the price to do so. We should not allow ourselves to be blinded by the traditions of men (Mark 7:1-13) that contradict God's Word, nor should we allow the fear of man to cause us to compromise the truth (John 12:42-43). We want to be faithful servants who follow our Lord Jesus Christ to do His will in all things. But in doing so, we must be careful to walk in grace, wisdom, and love and be patient with those who disagree. (Titus 3:2; 2 Tim. 2:23-24)

A CLOSING WORD

> *But the manifestation of the Spirit is given to each one for the profit of all... to another the working of miracles, to another prophecy, to another discerning of spirits, to another different kinds of tongues...*
>
> —1 CORINTHIANS 12:7, 10A

My objective has been to encourage and help the reader to enter the presence of God in a deeper experience of intercessory prayer and praise. I imagine my primary audience has been those who are spiritually hungry, those who sense a call to intercession, and those who possess a certain insight into prayer and God's presence. A few readers may have joined us who were simply curious about the topic. In any case, I trust the study has been helpful, informative, and enlightening. I also pray it has motivated you to pursue a deeper level of prayer and intercession that is so desperately needed in the world today.

If I pray in a tongue, my spirit prays.

—1 CORINTHIANS 14:14

For he who speaks in a tongue does not speak to men, but to God…

—1 CORINTHIANS 14:2A

For you indeed, give thanks well…

—1 CORINTHIANS 14:17A

Likewise the Spirit also helps in our weaknesses. For we do not know what we should pray for as we ought, but the Spirit Himself makes intercession for us…

—ROMANS 8:26A

CPSIA information can be obtained
at www.ICGtesting.com
Printed in the USA
FOW02n0857151116
29402FF

9 781940 024899